$12.95 (US)

Leading The Revolution

Angel Tuccy
Eric Reamer

Copyright ©2010
Leading The Revolution
Angel Tuccy & Eric Reamer
www.ExperiencePros.com

Published December, 2010

ISBN 10: 1456486357
ISBN-13/EAN-13: 978-1456486358

All rights reserved.

Photography by Joel Silverman
www.JoelSilverman.com

ALSO BY ANGEL TUCCY

Lists That Saved My Life

**Sex, Drugs & Rock N Roll:
3 Keys For A Healthier Lifestyle**

**Sex, Drugs & Rock N Roll:
90-Day Companion Journal**

ALSO BY ERIC REAMER AND ANGEL TUCCY

Lists That Saved My Business

**SUPER-Marketing
Audio Seminar**

Dedication

We dedicate this book to all those who dare to dream, and in the pursuit of their dreams, help others realize their dreams.

Leading The Revolution

Table of Contents

AUTHORS' NOTE 9
THE BUSINESS OF CUSTOMER SERVICE 13
WHY COLD CALLS… ARE COLD 15
FORGET ABOUT COLD CALLS 20
KEEP YOUR CUSTOMERS LOOKING 23
TOO MUCH OF A GOOD THING? 24
WHAT TO AVOID WHEN SENDING AN EMAIL 27
WRITE THE PERFECT HANDWRITTEN NOTE 30
YOU WOULDN'T "TRY-ON" A PARACHUTE 33
SMART MARKETING 36
SOCIAL FEEDIA – FEEDING YOUR SALES FUNNEL 38
FILLING YOUR PIPELINE WITH IDEAL CUSTOMERS ..40
RISKY BUSINESS 43
CUSTOMER SERVICE IS NOT A DEPARTMENT 45
IS FREE REALLY THE NEW PRICE TAG? 48
DON'T ADD COSTS UNLESS IT ADDS VALUE 50
INCLUDE GRATITUDE IN YOUR MARKETING PLAN ...52
YOUR PRESENCE HAS VALUE 54
COMMON SENSE… UNCOMMON PRACTICE 56
DON'T BLAME THE ECONOMY 58
ACT LIKE THE BOSS IS SHOWING UP 61
YOUR CUSTOMER WANTS A PERSONAL INVITATION ..63
BAD ECONOMY OR POOR CUSTOMER SERVICE? 66

WHO'S IN YOUR PASSENGER SEAT?	72
NETWORKING DRIVE-BY	75
DON'T FORGET TO SEND THE INVITATIONS	79
GETTING PAST THE GATEKEEPER	82
SURE-FIRE EXTREME CUSTOMER SERVICE	84
INVEST IN PEOPLE	90
ONE CAMPAIGN LEADS TO ANOTHER	94
YOUR CUSTOMER – FRIEND OR FOE?	96
WHAT TO DO IF THE SKY IS FALLING	100
PRETTY ISN'T ALWAYS PINK	103
BUSINESS ETIQUETTE	107
EMAIL ETIQUETTE	109
RSVP ETIQUETTE WILL GROW YOUR BUSINESS	113
THE ETIQUETTE OF NETWORKING	115
BUSINESS BY THE NUMBERS	119
5 WAYS TO DRIVE CUSTOMER LOYALTY	121
3 WAYS TO STAY IN TOUCH	124
10 WAYS TO BOOST YOUR ENERGY	126
5 WAYS TO APPRECIATE YOUR CUSTOMERS	129
10 TIPS FOR PREPARING FOR BUSINESS	132
8 BENEFITS TO HOLDING A WORKSHOP	135
7 TIPS FOR ATTRACTING NEW CUSTOMERS	138
3 STEPS TO EXTREME CUSTOMER SERVICE	141
7 WAYS TO CREATE EXTREME CUSTOMER SERVICE	145
4 PROSPECTING TIPS FOR NETWORK MARKETING	151
CLOSING THOUGHTS	154

Leading The Revolution

Authors' Note

The last year has been an amazing journey for us at Experience Pros. Just twelve months ago, we started a brand new radio show, airing daily on AM 560 KLZ Radio in Denver. Now we have archives of hundreds of shows with guests ranging from a Sr. Vice President of Microsoft to a variety of authors on every imaginable business topic, to entrepreneurs just getting their start in a new career path.

We graduated our first two Experience Pros University (EPU) classes this year, and started classes three, four and five. EPU is our comprehensive business development training program designed to help owners, managers and sales people create word-of-mouth marketing and achieve exponential growth through their existing customer base.

Angel published her first book, "Lists That Saved My Life", and we watched it hit the Amazon.com bestseller's list in four categories shortly thereafter. She has been asked to speak on the topic of pursuing your dreams while maintaining balance by women's groups all over.

Eight months later, our second book, "Lists That Saved My Business" was an instant success, and also achieved the bestseller's list on Amazon. SmallBusinessTrends.com subsequently nominated it for the Small Business Book of the Year.

We published our first audio seminar, "SUPER-Marketing", and it has been instrumental in helping several small business owners develop their marketing without having to invest a ton of money and resources that are in short supply when you're just getting started in a new business.

Right on the heels of that project, Angel collaborated with Dr. Nick Caras, a Chiropractor and wellness guru on her third book, "Sex, Drugs & Rock N Roll – 3 Keys For A Healthier Lifestyle". This book turns the old mantra of the sixties party lifestyle into the new mantra of wellness and nutrition for this decade. Along with the book, Dr. Nick and Angel published a 90-Day Companion Journal that helps readers stay focused and inspired.

One might be tempted to ask, "Where in the world would you find the time, effort and energy to write a fourth book within this calendar year?" And that is a fair question. The answer lies within the very pages of the book you are reading now, as this book is much more of a compilation.

We write and speak on the topic of Extreme Customer Service and business development every day at Experience Pros. We write for newspapers, journals, magazines and blogs. The articles that make up this book are all taken from our own blog, wwww.ExperienceProsBlog.com.

Readers of our book, "Lists That Saved My Business", our radio show listeners and students of Experience Pros University will see familiar thoughts and concepts, as in many cases, our blog articles represent the starting block for the philosophical positions that we espouse through our training.

And while there are some repetitive concepts between books, and in some cases, between the articles in this book themselves – we have chosen to leave them right where they are, because repetition is a solid tool for taking a message from short-term memory to long-term belief leading to game-changing action.

This book then, becomes more of a tool for you to use than a tome for you to read. It offers short segments of thought on business specific concepts that lay the foundation for your own thought development. It is divided into three sections, "The Business Of Customer Service", "Business Etiquette", and "Business By The Numbers". No article takes more than a couple of minutes to read, and yet all of them have the ability to spark thought into action in your business.

This is a behind-the-scenes look into our hearts and minds. We've left the articles in the voice in which they were written. These are first-person accounts of life, as it happens, to both of us, and how we filter that through our collaborative efforts at Experience Pros.

We hope you find validation, inspiration and motivation within the pages of this book. From there, we hope you are motivated to put into action the things that inspire you. And in the end, we hope to hear back from you with all of your great stories of success and customer-forward experiences.

The Business Of Customer Service

Why Cold Calls... Are Cold

Operator... Well could you help me place this call? – Jim Croce

Recently, a friend forwarded an article that was written all about "heating up cold calls". The article promised to offer three tips to get people to listen, respond, and buy! Sounds captivating, doesn't it? And I imagine for anyone who (has to make) cold calls in their line of work, the title and promise would simply be too wonderful to avoid reading on. I, on the other hand, do not make cold calls – ever. And yet, like a moth to flame, I was drawn in... I read the article. And now, I am writing one of my own!

It is well documented via our seminars, daily radio show and bestselling book, *Lists That Saved My Business*, that Angel Tuccy and I, owners of Experience Pros and professional business trainers, do not endorse cold calling.

We do, however, acknowledge that many people know of no other way to get the word out about their product or service, and so they resort to what they know. There is nothing inherently wrong with this. We also acknowledge that across the span of time, you will see the typical 1% to 4% rate of return that cold calling yields.

The article that was sent to me, however, provided far more questions than answers – and so I wish to address them in the chronological order in which they were presented.

Right out of the gate, the author states, "Let's face it, nobody really enjoys making cold calls and certainly nobody likes getting them." She should have stopped right there, and I would have been the first to offer a standing ovation of approval for a consistent, comprehensive and conclusive thought.

Such was not to be the case, however, as the very next sentence provided the first of several fatal flaws in logic and thought process that left me (and I suspect, several of her readers) frustrated. She wrote, "But they are a part of doing business, and they're not going away any time soon."

They may be a part of the author's way doing business... but as already stated, they are not a part of the way we do business. Is our business any less "valid" than hers? I suggest not. Do we have an alternative methodology of doing business? You bet!

I find a breakdown in consistent thought right from the get-go. "Everyone hates cold calling, and everyone hates receiving cold calls, so let me teach you how to make cold calls." Really? That would be similar to me saying, "Everyone hates cutting off their hand at the wrist, and nobody wants you to cut off your hand at the wrist, so let me teach you the best way to cut your hand off at the wrist." It just doesn't add up.

Now get this: I agree... yes, AGREE, with many of the points raised in the heart of the article. She writes: "cold calling is dreaded", "traditional selling is a shotgun approach", and even (this might surprise you) "done well, cold calling can work". I agree with all of this. We've never said cold calling doesn't work... but we offer an alternative that yields, on average, a 75-80% HIGHER ROI. I can *walk* to work... but if I want to get there TODAY, it might be better for me to take some form of transportation with a MOTOR, you know?

In the article, as promised, the author offers three "top tips" for cold calling success. Unfortunately, each of these points are less "tips" for success... as they are "what not to do's". And as such, they leave the readers semi-informed, but ill equipped to move forward. I will attempt to pick up the ball where the author left off, and suggest a positive course of action where none exists otherwise.

1. The author writes: "Focus on the goal, not the sale. Every cold call isn't about the sale!" (I agree.) And "Establish a relationship and gain trust with the contact first."

WHAT?

You – a TOTAL stranger – are calling the contact – another TOTAL stranger – and you're instructed to establish a relationship and gain trust... but nowhere are you told HOW that might happen... and that is because in the real world – that DOESN'T happen... ever. Relationships and trust are built over time – not in a 1 minute phone call. And what about the motive of your phone call? Are we really to accept that your motive is to start a relationship and establish trust, when the very premise of the call is to do so in order to gain a sale? Time for an integrity check.

2. The author writes: "You should never ask, 'is this a good time to talk?' or 'do you have a second?' or 'how are you today?' When you ask those questions, it creates instant

resistance; the walls go up, and the opportunity goes down." (I agree... almost) In the context of making cold calls, I agree that these questions are completely out of context, as there has been no relationship developed. These are questions that would be asked of someone "familiar"... someone who already knows you, and for whom you are asking out of respect for them and their time. These questions, therefore... have no place in the context of a cold call.

Nowhere, however, does the author offer you what you SHOULD ask or say.

3. The author writes: "Prepare and practice. Prepare the same way you would if you were making a presentation or delivering a speech. Then practice it out loud and practice several sales scenarios. Make it about them, always."

This is, perhaps, the most egregious "tell" of the entire piece, and it undermines the purported spirit of the article. In essence, it sums up the whole thought like this: No one likes to make cold calls, and everyone hates receiving them. That notwithstanding, go ahead and make them, because that's how business (i.e. sales) is done. Don't try to sell when you make cold calls, but just try to make friends. In the process of making friends, don't ask questions that can derail the sales process (that you're not engaging in), and make sure your sales pitch (that you're not making) is practiced and smooth, so that it doesn't "sound" scripted (though it is).

Does this resonate with your spirit??

Here's what we teach at Experience Pros:

1. YOU are perhaps the worst person to sell your product or service.

Of course you are going to tell me how wonderful you and your product or service is… I expect you to. But of FAR more value to me, a potential customer, is the voice of your EXISTING customer(s). I want to hear from them… not you.

2. Cold calling, while an established method of generating sales… yields such a small rate of return on investment, that we suggest developing the relationships that you have ALREADY started with your existing customer database. Imagine what you would be able to accomplish if you could recoup some 6 hours in your day – every day – because instead of mass marketing to a group of people that are not your target market… you leveraged your time and efforts with people who not only already buy from you – but are likely to associate with others who are also interested in your product or service.

3. Call on people who are likely to pick up the phone when they see it's you who are on the other line. Add value to them – not in a covert attempt to get a sale, but because you are genuinely interested and invested in them and their lives. People don't want to be sold… but they do want to buy. Your genuine, heart-felt touch is often met with THEM initiating a sale, because people do business with people they like and trust.

There are many, many more scenarios that one could cover on the topic of why cold calls are… cold. I will leave it at this for today, but if you just can't wait to learn more, allow me to encourage you to pick up a copy of our book, "Lists That Saved My Business", where we go into great detail on how to develop a thriving business, by building thriving relationships!

Forget About Cold Calls

If the phone doesn't ring... it's me. – Jimmy Buffet

Too often, the only phone calls I receive are cold calls. Forget about cold calls. Try using the phone for a more favorable activity. I'm referring to picking up the phone to follow up from a previous conversation or to extend an invitation to a client or business associate. I see a lot of people making lists of "things to do" or even using their automated CRM tool to remind them to make phone calls, but it seems like this one task gets pushed to bottom of the list over and over again. We would prefer to send an email or Facebook message to picking up the telephone. Since the invention of sales calls, the telephone has been getting heavier and heavier to the point of avoidance. You used to be able to use the phone to sell anything, but now, you need to use the phone to build a connection. Don't put off calling that client (you know who I'm talking about), pick up the phone and make a call that starts a conversation.

Right now, if you were to make a list of people you need to follow up with, you could easily come up with more than a dozen names. Even when sales are down, it seems so much easier to send an email. Don't underestimate the power your voice has in connecting with your clients. People do business with people, and your voice is a very powerful part of your brand. When you pick up the telephone to extend an invitation or to follow up with a client, you help them to relax about your calls. If the only time they hear from you is for a sales pitch, then of course, they will start to avoid you. But if you get into the habit of making phone calls and leaving voicemails, you'll actually earn more repeat business and train your clients to take your calls.

Here's how to use the phone in your favor.

1. Don't make a sales pitch over the phone. Do this in person.

2. Use the telephone to make appointments and email to confirm appointments. This is great for sending written directions or a link to your map.

3. Have a prepared 30-second message that includes your name, business, reason for call and the action (if any) you want them to take. Then hang up. This is not the time to ramble. And even if you are a thousand percent positive that they already have your phone number, it's a good idea to leave it again anyways. As a courtesy, leave your phone number at the beginning of your message instead of just at the end. This way, they can save the message, and only have to listen to the beginning to capture your number.

4. Get in the habit of inviting clients to events. These can be networking events, seminars, ribbon cuttings… you name it. An invitation allows you to call on your customers and get them excited about hearing from you. So often, when you call on a client, it's to get something from them. By extending an invitation, you are offering something to them.

5. Another great habit to form is calling on your clients just to check in. Maybe you haven't seen them in awhile and your typical plan of action is to send a postcard. By extending this personal touch, you increase your chances of seeing them again and getting more business back in the door. This goes a long way in creating loyal customers. And isn't that what we're really after?

How about calling and following up on that sale you didn't get? Chances are, if they shopped around and ended up buying someplace else, that other company didn't follow up, so here's a chance for your business to stand out and shine.

Don't worry about lost business or what you didn't do yesterday. Take today by storm. Pick up the phone and make that call. Your customers will be happy to hear from you, because every other call they received today was a cold call.

Keep Your Customers Looking

What's in a name? That which we call a rose
By any other name would smell as sweet.
– William Shakespeare

Seeing your own name in lights is a big dream for a lot of people. Using that information, you can create an overwhelming, yet subconscious, emotion in your customers by personalizing your information to them.

Personalized newsletters and emails have an increased rate of return. Emails and newsletters are more likely to be read and more time will be spent on a web page when your name is listed, versus when it's not. Psychologically, your customers are drawn to their own name. By including their name in the text, you keep their attention longer and have more chances of creating a sale by simply using your customer's name.

Use their name, and you'll keep your customers looking – at YOU.

Too Much Of A Good Thing?

Nothing. In excess. – Greek Proverb

We all agree that customer service is a good thing. Some would even say that more is better when it comes to connecting with your customers. But is it possible to overdo "customer service"? Is it possible to drive business AWAY by doing and saying all the right things?

Randy was looking for a pair of running shoes. He knew exactly what type of shoes he wanted. He knew what color, what style, even what brand he was looking for. He jumped into his car, and drove himself to the local shoe store, where he knew they would carry the exact pair of shoes that he wanted to buy.

Upon his entrance into the establishment, an employee who asked, "Can I help you find something", immediately greeted him.

"Nope. I've got it… thanks", said Randy amiably.

As he moved his way toward the men's department, he was met by another helpful employee who inquired, "Can I help you find something?"

"Nope. I've got it... thank you", replied Randy.

Working his way into the aisle that featured his size shoes, Randy met yet another employee. "Can I help you find something?", came the employee's now-predictable query.

Slightly irritated now, Randy replied, "Nope. I've got it." The employee moved on, and Randy found the pair of shoes he was looking for. As he was trying on the shoes, yet another employee came around the corner and with no apparent observation skills, asked a now redundant question... "Can I..."

"NOPE. I've GOT IT", came Randy's noticeably frustrated reply. Shaking his head and trying to shrug off what was becoming an abrasive onslaught of mindless, robotic, one-track lines from the employees, he started to put the shoes back in the box with the intent to make his purchase and get out of the store as quickly as possible.

Such was not to be the case, however, as just as he was nearing the checkout counter, the original employee that greeted him at the front door noticed him, and asked, "Can I help you find something?" Randy handed the employee the box of shoes... the shoes that he WANTED to purchase... and as he continued on toward the exit, he curtly replied... "NOPE. I've GOT IT."

Lest you succumb to the desire to believe that this is an improbable story, let me assure you that Randy is a very real person – and his story happened exactly as was recounted here. And everyone in business stands to benefit from the lesson found within the lines above: there most certainly is such a thing as "too much of a good thing".

On the surface, none of the employees did anything wrong. They had obviously been instructed to approach customers with an offer to assist them in finding the right pair of shoes. Anyone in business would agree that such an offer of help is the right thing to do.

The wheels came off, however, as it became crystal clear that there was no variance for the multiple attempts to be helpful – and further, there was no communication between employees as it related to the customer in question. Instead, the automaton-like repetition of the exact same question, by not one – but every one of the employees (and even twice by one of them) was enough to frustrate the customer to the point of overriding his desire to purchase the shoes in question.

What could have changed the outcome of this scenario? A little variety would have gone a long way. A global awareness of who had already offered assistance, and a sensitivity to the mounting frustration of the customer would have diffused a tense situation. Had any one of these suggestions come into play, Randy would have purchased his shoes, and the shoe store would have made an easy sale.

Is there such a thing as "too much of a good thing?" You bet there is. Perhaps a more important question is… what are you doing to avoid it?

What To Avoid When Sending An Email

I don't believe in email. I'm an old fashioned girl. I prefer calling and hanging up. – Carrie Bradshaw

Email can be a powerful tool to connect with your customers, if it's used in a genuine way. Avoid some common email mistakes and you'll increase your chances of your emails being read. For help with email etiquette, read Email Etiquette often and share it with your co-workers.

In the world of Email, avoid common, yet easily avoidable, mistakes.

Do not use email to make a decision or conduct a conversation; too much is left up to interpretation.

Do not attach unnecessary files. Even innocently, your attachments could annoy your customers, cause a breakdown in their email system or be a cocoon for hidden viruses.

Do not overuse the High Priority option or the words Urgent and Important. Remember, your failure to plan does not constitute an emergency on their part. More often, you come across as being aggressive and unorganized.

Do not write in all CAPITALS because it translates as shouting. If you really are shouting at the person, you should re-think using email as your communication source.

Do not put it in writing unless it's okay for anyone to read it. Sending an email is like passing a note in school. If you don't want your email to be displayed on a bulletin board, don't send it. Moreover, never make any sexist or racially discriminating comments in emails, even if they are meant to be a joke. Email is not confidential.

Do not use abbreviations and emoticons in business emails. The recipient might not be aware of the meanings of the abbreviations BTW (by the way) and LOL (laugh out loud) and in business emails these are generally not appropriate. The same goes for emoticons, such as the smiley :-) . If you are not sure whether your recipient knows what it means, it is better not to use it.

Do not forward chain letters. We can confidently say that they are all are hoaxes. Delete the letters as soon as you receive them.

Do not request delivery and read receipts. This will almost always annoy your recipient before they have even read your message. If you want to know whether an email was received, it is better to ask.

Do not ask to recall a message. Most likely your message has already been delivered and read. It is better just to send an email to say that you have made a mistake. This will look much more honest than trying to recall a message.

Do not forward virus hoaxes. If you receive an email message warning you of a new unstoppable virus that will immediately delete everything from your computer, this is most probably a hoax. By forwarding hoaxes you use valuable bandwidth and sometimes virus hoaxes contain viruses themselves, by attaching a so-called file that will stop the dangerous virus. Even if the content seems to be bona fide, the senders are usually not.

Do not reply to spam. By replying to spam or by unsubscribing, you are confirming that your email address is 'live'. Confirming this will only generate even more spam. Therefore, just hit the delete button or use email software to remove spam automatically.

Write The Perfect Handwritten Note

*I believe the handwritten note
has become a status symbol. – Julie Weiss*

When working on your marketing campaign to connect with more customers and bring more sales to your door, there is one perfect sales flyer you can send. It doesn't require a large PR firm to create a catchy headline. It doesn't require a gimmick that looks like an item from the government or a huge increase in your marketing budget. In fact, you can even put your company logo on the outside and it is still guaranteed to be opened, read and acted upon.

The very best item you can send to your customers is a handwritten note card. It's not the trendy new thing, in fact, it's a little old-fashioned. And, it's exactly what your customer is looking for from you.

You are asking your customers to change their habits or their pattern to come and do business with you. Make it personal and you'll show them that their business really matters to you.

Here is how to write the perfect note card that gets opened, read and acted upon.

Use a blank note card with your logo imprinted on the outside. This is a great opportunity to create trust with your brand. A picture is memorable and you want your customers to remember your brand.

Handwrite the note. If your handwriting is illegible, hire this out. It's okay if you don't like your own handwriting. Most people are their own worst critic, but your handwritten note conveys your personality. You can hand write a note on your business stationery and leave the typed notes for a more formal conversation. People do business with people – and your customers will overlook your handwriting in favor of the message you are sharing.

Send notes right away and often. Each day, make it a point to send a card to everyone you interact with. Even if a customer calls for a price quote and they purchase somewhere else, a handwritten card thanking them for the opportunity is 'going the extra mile' in customer service.

Open with enthusiasm. The recipient wants to hear that you enjoyed the gift, the meeting or the event. 'Dear Sue, I really enjoyed our conversation / the comment you shared with me / spending time with you / the referral you shared."

Compliment the recipient. Compliments are few and far between. You handwritten appreciation will most likely be stored away and treasured. Describe how they have made an impact on your day or a decision. Emphasize the person, not the milestone.

Don't stress about making every note unique. It's okay to use a template when writing out many notes at once. Personalize at least one sentence in the note and you'll find that you may end up being thanked for your handwritten note.

Don't ask for a sale and don't sell anything. Don't add "by the way, I appreciate your referrals" or "I'd really like to earn your business". This is obvious to your customer and saying so only changes the intention of the card. Customers already know how to refer you and talk about you. By sending the card and leaving out the sales pitch, your customer will display the card and show it off. It is acceptable to include your business card in the note.

Handwrite the address and put a real stamp on it. This conveys that you took the time to be thoughtful and guarantees that your note will be opened and read. Add your return address, including your logo and company name. You can even order stamps with your company logo on it. The more impressions you can create, the more trust you are building.

Keep stationery and stamps handy. Spending a few minutes during the day writing cards is easy to fit in – if you are prepared for it. If you need to start a new habit, schedule it into your day.

Follow up with a phone call to set an appointment or to take them through the next step in your sales process. If this is a potential customer, don't wait for them to respond.

Most handwritten cards are displayed and shared with others. Still, other cards are tucked away and saved forever. An email might be good enough, but email doesn't convey a connection. When you really want to connect with your customers, send the perfect handwritten card.

You Wouldn't "Try-On" A Parachute

Life in the twentieth century is like a parachute jump. You have to get it right the first time. – Margaret Mead

10,000 feet... There you are cruising comfortably among the clouds when much to your surprise the pilot of your airplane straps on his parachute, urges you to do the same, and then pops the door and jumps! This scenario is not much different than when you find yourself in a small business that has just received news of challenging times ahead. Whether it's the economy, or staffing issues, or a difficult cash flow situation – there IS a solution! Your parachute is sitting just over there...

In many cases, however, business owners make the critically flawed mistake of viewing the solution (the parachute) as a suggestion. Much like shopping for a new outfit, the tendency is to "try on" various ideas until we find one that makes us comfortable – rather than realizing the overall value of the solution itself. Think it not so? Let's look at a few case studies.

Case Study #1: You're new to the business community, and need to generate new customers. You were told that the local Chamber of Commerce was your solution, so you pony up and pay your dues. Over the next several months you attend networking events and hand out tons of business cards. But your phone isn't ringing, and you start to feel like you were given bad information. Your parachute straps are a little too tight, so you decide to take it off. Key indicators: You stop attending as many functions, and you start using phrases like, "I tried that... it didn't work for me."

Case Study #2: Your business is established, but it's hit a plateau. You've been told that ABC Consulting is fabulous, and so you decide to hire ABC to take you to the next level. The workload placed upon you is considerable – especially since you need to do that in addition to running your business. You start to fall behind, and with every passing week you feel more and more burdened. Your parachute is too heavy, so you take it off. Key indicators: You discontinue your consulting service and use phrases like, "it's too expensive."

Case Study #3: Your business is barely afloat. Existence is more like survival, and you wonder where your next paycheck will come from. Someone keeps encouraging you to "pay it forward" by encouraging, supporting, and helping other business owners achieve their goals, but all you can see is the mounting stack of bills and obstacles in your own business. The parachute is simply one more thing – and you can't take anything else... so you refuse to even put it on. Key Indicators: You are paralyzed by the tidal wave of debt and the trickle of customers. You use phrases like, "Why isn't everyone else helping ME?"

My friends, in each one of these real-life scenarios – the parachute has made itself known to you, and yet for one reason – (excuse) – or another, you've found a way to snatch failure from the jaws of success! Is it that you are afraid – truly fearful – of success? That's possible. Many people do not have the infrastructure to handle real success. But more often the case isn't one of fear of success – but it is one of lack of understanding the overall value of the parachute. You wouldn't "try on" a parachute at the moment it is needed... you would strap that thing on and ride it all the way to the end!

If you find yourself in any of the scenarios provided – or perhaps a scenario all your own – and a parachute of one type or another has been offered to you... don't go into it with the attitude, "I'll try this, and if it doesn't work for me – I'll try the next thing." Rather – pick your course of action, and see it to the end. What's the old adage? Failing to plan is planning to fail!

Safe landings!

Smart Marketing

There is a place in the world for any business that takes care of its customers – after the sale. – Harvey MacKay

When it comes to sales and marketing for your company, YOU are not the best person to be selling for your business. No need to panic; you have a database full of capable sales people. Your existing database is your gold mine to new prospects. If you know anything about panning for gold, you know that you have to sift through a lot of sand before you strike it rich. You've already done that. Your database is full of people who have already bought from you. They already like you and trust you – and you've set the foundation for creating loyal customers, but you're not doing enough after the sale. Truly great customer service and loyal customers comes from following up after the sale. You've already sifted through all of the no's and found your yes's. Rather than focus all of your marketing efforts on obtaining new customers and strangers, the smart way to market your business is to train your team to hold onto the customers you already have.

In a typical sales process, once a transaction is complete, the next step is to do a 180-degree turn to find your next sale. It's exciting to nurture and court your customer when there's hope of getting the deal, but before their signature is even dry, you're already thinking about how to get to that next customer.

Yet, the answer is standing in front of you, probably still with a pen in their hand.

Every customer interaction is a chance to create a memorable experience that will get your customers bragging about you. Most customers, even though satisfied, will not tell anyone. That means that you aren't earning any referrals from them. This doesn't mean that you forgot to ask for a list of ten names and numbers, it means that you left such an impression that your customer bragged about you.

Rather than focus all of your marketing efforts on obtaining new customers and strangers, train your team to hold onto the customers you already have. A car salesman tried this. He knew that his customers weren't going to by another car from him the following month, so he was skeptical about following up so soon. He now makes phone calls to check in on his previous months customers. These phone calls aren't sales calls. They are genuine phone calls of sincerity. More often than not, these conversations turn into more referrals, even though he doesn't ask for them. They are willingly offered because this salesman takes time to say "thank you". For most consumers, a genuine "thank you" is worth far more than gold.

That's smart marketing.

Social Feedia – Feeding Your Sales Funnel

I started the site when I was 19. I didn't know much about business back then. – Mark Zuckerberg

Over 30 million business pages now exist on Facebook alone, not to mention, the other five dozen or so, social media sites. Most businesses we come across are just hobbyists – hacking away at their computer all day long versus going out and interacting with their potential customers. But there are some successful corporations making a strong impact with their customers. Can your business realistically use to feed your own sales funnel?

The typical sales process includes multiple ways of prospecting that provides you with enough information to contact them later. This can include a random collection of business cards, asking an existing client or prospect for a list of people to call, trading contact information in exchange for some small token of value, or obtaining a list of "your" target market, just to name a few. Sales training often includes multiple ways to to collect a name, email address and/or phone number.

Once the target information is in your database, you get to use this information to push them through your sales funnel. This process is flawed from the very beginning, because everyone knows that these contacts aren't really your target market and there's only a four percent chance of turning any one of these contacts into a closed transaction.

The use of social media feeds the search engine tools and has the ability to bring your organic search, that is an unpaid sponsor spot, higher up the search pages. When you search for your business name, no doubt your website comes up, but you can also see any comments or listings on other sites you participate in such as Facebook, Meetup, and LinkedIn.

If you search for certain keywords, such as customer service, you will find the businesses who are using social media will be ever-present on the search pages. This is where the roles are reversed and customers are finding their way into your sales funnel. Customers are also looking for prospects. Your business is a prospect for a customer. Social media can feed your sales funnel with customers who are looking specifically for you!

Everyday, customers are searching the web for computer training, customer service, and how to use social media. If your company isn't feeding the social media sites, you are letting your sales funnel go hungry.

Filling Your Pipeline With Ideal Customers

Attempting to fill your pipeline by cold calling or buying a list is a "funnel-damental" problem. – Eric Reamer

You're told to fill your customer pipeline with as many prospective customers as possible. The idea behind this theory is that when you have a full pipeline, then you have more true customers coming out. Do you believe that is really how it works? I doubt that if you fill your pipeline with non-customers, then ideal customers will come out. The truth is, you don't really want it all, nor do you have to have it all. You don't need a full pipeline to have true customers – you need a filtering system to filter out non-customers. If you're busy and out amongst people, then you meet enough people day in and day out that aren't really prospective customers. You know it, and they know it, but aren't you told that you're supposed to add every new person you meet into your pipeline? These days, there are filters for everything. You can buy filtered water, filters for your coffee and filters for your air. You can add filters to software programs, shows on cable television and to block unwanted phone calls.

We use filters to make sure we're left with only the purest, finest of what we are truly interested in. Can you filter out customers?

If it's true that the person you are, is in direct correlation to the people you associate with and the books you read, then it becomes really important to filter out people. You filter the books you read by either judging them by their cover or their reviews and listening to recommendations. Even as your social network grows, you filter out with whom you spend time. But in business, you have taken a completely open mentality in believing that everyone you meet is a prospect or potential customer. You collect business cards from people you barely know. You call on people either in person, with your newsletters or direct mail campaigns, thinking that he with the most number of contact wins the game. Is it really a numbers game, or should you be much pickier about the filters you are using?

When I think of filters, I think of the different mesh size that filters come in. When I'm choosing programs for my children to watch, that filter becomes a very small, tight weave. But when I'm choosing customers to call on, suddenly, it seems like the world is telling me to use a chain link fence with a gaping hole, and pretty much anyone who breathes is acceptable.

Why do we buy into the formula that tells us it takes 100 contacts to close one deal? If we are talking to everyone who breathes, then yes, it will take 100 people to reject us before we can make a sale. But what if our filters were tighter and the mesh was much smaller? If we were pre-qualifying people we meet with a clearer image of what makes up our ideal customer, then we could practically remove rejection from our sales process. How great would that be?

By clearly identifying your ideal customer – you can effectively market to only them. Your advertising dollars are clearly invested and you will see a greater return on your dollar. Your sales team stops wasting time meeting with people who aren't able to make decisions. You aren't sending out mailers to unknown addresses.

Take some time to create a clear picture of whom your ideal customer is. Where do they live and work? What are the common denominators that your best customers share? Create a conversation and a relationship with your ideal customers, and focus on their hot buttons. Filter out the unwanted, the undesirable, and the uninterested. Create a filter that leaves you with only the finest, purest customer and let the debris fall away.

Risky Business

Behold the turtle. He makes progress only when he sticks his neck out. – James Bryant Conant

The number one obstacle to building your business into a thriving entity may surprise you. In a world predisposed to pointing fingers and making excuses, we, as a general rule, overlook the biggest offender, the main reason for our lackluster sales... to quote author Walt Kelly, "We have met the enemy, and he is us."

We live in a society that measures our success by the number of transactions that we generate, rather than the number of people that we help. And as a result of the pressure to perform, we actually become our own worst enemy by developing a "transaction mentality" instead of a "value added" intent. We all agree that people want to buy, but that they don't want to be sold... and yet, in the very next breath, we sell, sell, sell. What's wrong with this picture? More to the point, how can we assess the illness, and prescribe the cure?

When you attempt to push a sale upon your customers, you must realize that they go instantly into defensive position, and have established tried and true responses to your efforts. They use phrases like, "no thanks, I'm just looking", and "how much does this cost?" They answer your advances with avoidance and objections, which are really just indications of their level of discomfort with the risks they perceive in doing business with you.

Your customers will react much more positively to you if you provide solutions to their objections – even before their objections surface. Here are a few solution phrases that can open doors by shifting the perspective from one of "how can I SELL you", to "how can I help you"...

- We offer:
- We match:
- We guarantee:
- We help:
- We can:

View yourself as a trusted advisor instead of a salesman/woman and watch your customers surprise you with their lifelong loyalty! Go ahead, give it a shot... you have everything to gain!

Customer Service Is Not A Department

Dream more than others think practical. Expect more than others think possible. Care more than others think wise. – Howard Schultz

The culture of customer service is becoming more and more extinct. Customer service should be a culture, not just a department. I just left the big, blue, mega-bank lobby near my home. I went inside to make a deposit. I'd like to recognize the people who work there and so I take the time to go inside the lobby and create some semblance of personal banking. Today, I did not accomplish any connection. In fact, I left the lobby fuming. I wasn't fuming because they treated me poorly – it was because I witnessed them treating another customer in such a rude manner, that frankly, I don't think I can continue to bank there.

While I was waiting in line, I was listening to the big, blue, mega-bank employee who was talking on the telephone at the end of the counter. She was talking in a raised tone, so anyone in the lobby could hear her side of the conversation clearly. If you weren't caught up in the volume of her voice, her eye-rolling made up for it. She rolled her eyes at the customer on the phone, while looking at me, as if I was her ally on discussing company policy out loud for other customers to hear.

Next, she interrupted my transaction to look up this customer's record to see who opened the account. Yes, she used the computer that was being used for my transaction with another teller. She was smug about the fact that she was defending company policy. Apparently, the big, blue, mega-bank has an overriding policy that says you cannot have your money the same day that you make your deposit. She blabbered on about something called "same-day availability".

I realize that policies are in place to protect your company and they are in place more for your protection than they are for your customers. But let me remind you of this: IT'S NOT YOUR MONEY!!!! That money belongs to your customer. She is calling you out of an immediate need and you won't give her own money to her. Poor customer service is becoming so commonplace in business, it's as if you've forgotten why you are in business in the first place, and that is to serve your customers. As Don Gallegos, past president of King Soopers said, "Win the customer, not the argument".

Here's my advice to the customer on the telephone: Close your account immediately and ask for ALL of your money, RIGHT NOW. It's your money. Take it to a bank that understands that.

I will be closing my accounts with this big, blue, mega-bank. I will tell them that I do not want to be the customer who calls on the phone asking for help to get my own money and be yelled at in front of other customers.

Look at your customer policies. If they don't benefit your customer, go back and re-write them. When your customer wins, so does your business. Train your employees to treat every customer, even the ones on the phone, as if they really matter to your company. It seems simple, but if you're losing customers, you don't need a department to take a survey to tell you why. Make customer service your company culture, and you'll retain loyal customers.

Yes, customer service is seemingly extinct, but I'm on the look out for those companies out there who are alive and thriving for their customers.

Is FREE Really The New Price Tag?

*Strive not to be a success,
but rather to be of value. – Albert Einstein*

These days, it seems like the only way to bring in a crowd of new customers is to offer something for free. Free is the buzzword that will always grab any consumer's attention. We all want something for nothing.

There is a new bakery in my neighborhood called "Rocky's Treats" and they sell the most decadent creme puffs. When they first opened, to get the word out, they advertised in a mailer with coupons for a free creme puff. No purchase necessary. The proprietor said that he got quite a few of those coupons turned in, but that those customers never came back.

The local NY Pizzeriaa in Centennial and Littleton started offering a similar method of tantalizing his customers. Watching the trends of Happy Hours and flowing libations, they decided to throw in a free bottle of wine with every $30.00 dinner purchase. You can't use any other coupons with this offer, but it's attractive for those who enjoy a glass of wine with their evening meal.

The owner figures that when a couple goes out to eat, the bar tab alone can be over $30.00 so this is an incredible savings for his customers. A lot of restaurants might throw in a free glass or a free dessert, but at the pizzeria in both Centennial and Littleton, he's offering the whole bottle for free.

Marketers know that the most powerful word in marketing is free. The word free draws in a crowd, but is that new business sustainable? Can you convert the customers who come in for something free to be loyal customers who will return later when the promotion ends?

Consumers tend to be skeptical of the giveaways these days because so often, there is a catch. The proverbial chase of "something for nothing" is out there, but mostly, consumers are like dogs chasing their tales. Most free promotions aren't that free.

Using the free term can be a great way to entice someone to try out your brand for the first time, but if that's where the enticement ends, then why would they return? When you have a customer in the presence of your brand – that is, in your store, interacting with your staff, enjoying their freebie, are you creating a memorable experience for them to brag about or even remember?

Use the free item to draw in the crowd, but once they are there, connect with your customers in a real way that gets them talking about you. Collect their contact information and use it to thank them for their business and for giving you a try. Handwrite those thank you's. Offer a customer experience that they can't find anywhere else. Be revolutionary, and you'll turn those free coupons into loyal customers.

Don't Add Costs Unless It Adds Value

You know you are getting old when the candles cost more than the cake. – Bob Hope

As a business professional, you are constantly being enticed by new ways to be successful and create profits. You want a profitable business. You want to offer extreme customer service. You want to improve the quality of your services with fewer mistakes and create more effective use of your time. It's easy to make those decisions, when you know how your business flows.

Ask yourself; does the decision flow with my business model?

There's an acronym to help you filter out your decisions on whether or not a new opportunity is a good investment for you. A helpful quote from Sakichi Toyoda, founder of the Toyota Motor Company helps bring decisions into a new perspective: "Don't add costs unless it adds value to your customer". To grow your business, your business must FLOW.

F – Friend or Foe. Is this good for my customer or will it alienate them? Can I go back to the drawing board and make this a win-win situation for my business and for my customer? If not, it's a waste and needs to be discarded or re-worked so the customer wins.

L – Leading the Way. Does this decision set me apart from my competition so it's better for my customers? Is it setting a good example for those who follow me? Does it lead the way for bragging customers?

O – Opportunity Costs. Is this a great opportunity for adding value to my customers? If I spend money on this decision, is it driving me away or leading me closer to my customer relationships? Sometimes, we need to forsake immediate returns in favor of long-term customer relationships. Benjamin Franklin said "A penny saved is a penny earned". The same is true for your customers; A customer saved, is a customer earned.

W – Worthwhile Use of Time. If it takes time and doesn't add value to your customers, it's a waste. Use your prime time for connecting with customers rather than with tasks that don't add value to them. Do you recognize your prime time hours for connecting with your customers?

Toyoda said "Everyone should tackle some great project at least once in their life. You should make an effort to complete something that will benefit society."

When you take the time to add value to individual consumers, you are adding value to society. When you help others, you create loyal customers, and that helps your business.

Include Gratitude In Your Marketing Plan

Handwritten cards never lose their luster, and a personalized note can make a powerful and positive impact on your customer. – Angel Tuccy

Sometimes, I sound like a broken record. Write thank you notes, write thank you notes, hand-write thank you notes. This is the most important piece of literature you can mail out to your customers, and yet everyone tells me that they don't do it. A hand-written thank you note is guaranteed to be opened by the recipient – and often, left out on their desk for themselves and others to see. A hand-written thank you note is guaranteed to be read by the intended, rather than filtered through by an assistant. A hand-written thank you note is one of the best ways to put your brand in front of your target market.

Yet, most business professionals admit to me that they are lacking in their follow up process for one reason or another. They tell me that the number one thing that they neglect to do is send thank you notes.

Even though we know it's the very easiest and best thing to do – it is the one thing we all neglect. I have a friend who tells me that he rarely sends thank you notes. However, when he first started his business, he did it all the time. His business grew and he got so busy that he doesn't have time to write them anymore. However, business has tapered off recently, and he came to me for advice. My advice to him is something I read on my shampoo bottle. This clever little phrase not only helped increase shampoo sales, but it's great advice for all business owners; Lather, Rinse, Repeat.

Lather your clients with thank you notes. Make them handwritten, and write something bubbly inside.

Rinse every interaction with your customers by sending them a handwritten thank you card. Rinse your brand over your customers in a way that makes them feel all squeaky clean. Don't dirty it up by asking for another sale or a referral – just rinse them with a thank you. Besides being a professional courtesy, a handwritten card says you care enough to take the time to send it.

Repeat it over and over again. Every interaction deserves a genuine follow up. A handwritten card has the potential to create trust and recognition. The gesture gives your customers a chance to talk about you. The average person will tell 3 people about a card they received and they will show it to 3 others.

Expressing gratitude should be one of the major components of your marketing plan. When you send thank you notes, you focus on the pleasant aspects of doing business. As a result, you are more aware of your success and you make it more pleasant to do business with you.

Lather, Rinse, Repeat reminds your customers that you're grateful for their business. Write thank you notes and you'll improve your business.

Your Presence Has Value

Presence is more than just being there. – Malcolm Forbes

I was a guest at a networking leads group and was enjoying the commentary going around the room as each person recited whom they had referred and done business with recently. It was inspiring to hear so many people add value to the others in the room by being walking testimonials for each other. I love hearing people brag about others they've done business with because it fits my philosophy that you are the worst person to be selling your product. Bragging clients are perceived to be far more trustworthy than your sales copy jargon.

The culture in the room changed though, when one person said that they had to nothing to add. I thought the statement was profound – and uncomfortable. My interpretation is that this fellow felt that because he hadn't conducted business with anyone in the room, that there was no further value to share – and I felt so strongly that his statement was false. Your presence adds value.

It's human nature to think the world revolves around you – but it's not all about you. When you are in a room with others, your presence has value. That value can be positive or negative – you are either adding or taking away. There is no neutral ground. You are either taking up space, or you are adding to the conversation.

You can add value to others simply with your presence. I was speaking with a friend who recently attended a funeral. So much value comes just by being present. Often, you don't have to DO anything, but be present, listen and care.

A – add something to the conversation rather than subtract. Offer a story, a memory, a quote or brag on someone else.

D – don't underestimate your contribution. Your presence adds value. If you don't feel like it does, read up on topics that are interesting to you and talk about them.

D – deliver the goods. Be prepared in advance with a headline or a piece of industry news. There are so many resources available online that you don't even have to make up stuff.

People connect with people – and we all have something to add. When you focus on adding value to others, your own value will increase.

Common Sense... Uncommon Practice

Common sense is not so common. - *Voltaire*

Angel and I attended a rather unique Business After Hours networking event last night. It was held at a mortuary. That's right... a mortuary. Dead people. Tombstones. Creepy, right? NOT AT ALL!

I have to say, it was one of the most wonderful, truly ALIVE events that we've been to – ever! Every detail was thought of and planned for. The catering was unbelievable! The location was immaculate and well-suited for a gathering. The staff were attentive and pleasant – truly pleasant to be around! The weather was amazing, and the turnout was impressive.

All of those attributes are probably to be expected. It was, after all, the largest gathering of the month for the particular group that we were with. But upon closer examination, the detail to attention started to show itself... all over the place!

The umbrella holders at every door... The tissue boxes at the end of every row of seats... The projector and screen... The webinars...? Yes... webinars! You see, this is a place where the statistic, 1 out of every 1 will die, is embraced as a very natural part of LIFE! And they have created an experience for when that happens, to truly CELEBRATE life!

Anticipating your customer's needs, and then meeting (or exceeding) them is what extreme customer service is all about. We live in a very spread-out country. Sometimes, when people pass – friends and relatives live hundreds... even thousands of miles away – and cannot get to the service at which the celebration of life and the process of healing and closure begins. So our friends at the Olinger Chapel Hills Cemetery go the extra mile – and bring the service to you – via the internet!

Now that, my friends... is common sense... and UNCOMMON practice!

I loved it! We had a great time! And yes... I can't wait to go back... to see the friends on this side of life again!

Don't Blame The Economy

My dog is worried about the economy because Alpo is up to 99 cents a can. That's almost $7.00 in dog money. – Joe Weinstein

I had a difficult customer experience today and it got me thinking about the different stores that I've stopped shopping at based on my customer experience. Right off the top of my head, without having to think long at all, I recalled three different stores that have lost my business due to poor customer service. They didn't lose me as a customer because of the economy; they lost me because they treated their customer poorly.

The first store that lost me as a customer was because every transaction seemed to have a discrepancy in their pricing. I would toss an item into my basket, and at the register, the wrong price would ring up. Having the correct price keyed-in required a lengthy process of a manager override. This happened on three or four occasions before I decided to stop shopping there. My decision was not based on the economy. They lost my business because of continued poor customer service.

The second store that lost my business has a return policy of 30 days or less. I struggled with a cashier over a return. I had bought a dress 32 days ago and I could not get a refund. The month had flown by and I missed their window. I had my receipt and all the tags were attached, but I walked out of the store with a dress I didn't want and I haven't been back. Over $62.00, they lost a regular customer. It had nothing to do with the economy, but I admit, my budget improved because I'm not regularly stopping in to see what I'm missing any more.

I had been a pretty loyal customer for quite awhile, often shopping with friends. I was really hoping that they would try to retain my business, because I really enjoyed shopping there. It would have been easy for them to keep my business – except that their policy was not a "customer-retaining" policy. I want to shop at stores where the only policy they have is to "exceed my expectations". If it's going to make my life difficult, poor economy or not, I'm shopping someplace else.

The third store that lost my business because of a poor customer experience also had a difficult return policy. Though I can't be sad. Saying good-bye to this store has really worked in my benefit because I was always buying stuff I didn't need, thinking that someday this great bargain or nifty little thing would come in handy. I can't even begin to tally up how many of my purchases at this store ended up in one of my donation bags or garage sales. This one had the biggest impact on my budget.

Whether or not the loss of my business has had a significant impact on the economy of these stores is uncharted. I'm certain that I'm not the only consumer changing my buying habits based on how I'm treated. If customers continue to be treated as dispensable, then the economy is going to falsely receive more and more blame. I am finding it harder and harder to find places to shop.

The sad part is that my business could have been retained if the stores were looking at their policies through the eyes of their customers. The good news is, the poor economy is helping me save money like never before.

Act Like The Boss Is Showing Up

Every day I get up and look through the Forbes list of the richest people in America. If I'm not there, I go to work. – Robert Orben

I was having coffee in a local coffee shop where they were anticipating a visit from their District Manager that afternoon. This was a scheduled visit, so they knew he was coming, and they knew what his expectations were for their store.

There was a lot of hustle and bustle straightening shelves and the countertops, clearing away the items that were out of place. Someone was washing the fingerprints off the door and another was emptying trashcans and straightening chairs.

I found the activity to be amusing. I am their customer. Really, when it comes down to it, I am the one who pays the rent and their paychecks. Maybe not me personally, but my activity keeps their doors open. Without customers, layoffs happen and cutbacks abound. Even though the coffee shop was full of paying patrons, we were not being given this special treatment. Even though it was during regular operating hours, when you expect customers to be arriving, the coffee shop was not anxious about extending the customers the same treatment that the DM would be receiving.

What behaviors show up when you know the "Boss" is coming in? Are you more aware of the way things look when you know an inspection is coming? Do you realize that even though they don't offer you a report or reprimand, your customers are inspecting you, too? Do you give your customers the same treatment that you extend to your DM? What if you are the boss? Who holds you accountable? Do you treat your customers as if they are the District Managers of your business?

Every customer is your boss. Straighten up for them. Put on a clean apron and give them the service of a lifetime. Your boss is watching. It's your customer.

Your Customer Wants A Personal Invitation

Never eat alone. – Keith Ferrazzi

One afternoon last week, my schedule was full of back-to-back meetings and events and I had a decision to make about squeezing in a networking event. I knew I would only be able to drop in for half an hour, and with only half the events of the day under my belt, I was toying with the idea of skipping it. However, it was my friend, Theresa Sanford, hosting the event and she had personally invited me.

Based on the personal invitation, I decided to go. I was in and out in thirty minutes, but made a valuable connection before I left, which turned out to be very worth my time. The 303Network holds monthly networking events that benefit local non-profit organizations and they draw in crowds of 300 + people. The secret? You might think that it's the fact that she posts the event on Meetup.com and Facebook and uses social media sites to promote.

You might think that it's because she sends out an email to her vast and growing database every couple of weeks. You might think that people just stumble across it by accident when they see the crowd growing and come in out of curiosity. The secret lies in the personal invitation that you get. Theresa has made it a point to connect and create a relationship with most of the people in the Denver Metro area. If you know Theresa, you are her friend. Theresa is constantly connecting with people and inviting them to her events. And it works.

Hosting a successful event is dependent on people showing up. While Experience Pros teaches you how to use invitations to grow your business, we tend to put more emphasis on the invitation rather than the event itself. We often tell people that it's okay if your guests say no, and encourage the fact that you invited them puts your brand back in their mind. However, if you are the host of an event, the value of attendance is great.

A personal invitation yields the greatest success in getting people to actually attend your party. It's important to post the details on a website or through Facebook and Meetup.com, but I suggest you use this as more of a reference, as opposed to getting people to actually commit to coming.

You don't have to call everyone you know, but definitely call the people you really want to be there. When you are out and about, invite the people you see, right there. Don't wait until you get back to your computer to send the notice, personally ask them to come along.

If you have several events, a personal invitation to each and every one may not be necessary, but if you really want to have butts in the seats or people paying at the door, your emphasis needs to be on personally inviting your guests.

If you don't have a strong enough relationship with someone to invite him or her to your event, you are at risk to losing him or her to your competition. Pick up the phone and call them.

Engage them in a conversation and make them feel as if you really want them there – because you do.

Without guests at an event, you've just thrown a lot of time and money out the window. Your personal invitation may just be the thing that sways them into showing up.

Bad Economy Or Poor Customer Service?

The superior man understands what is right. The inferior man understands what will sell. - Confucius

In the strip mall near my house, there are an unusually high number of empty retail spaces available. It seems as if some shops close as quickly as they open. Whenever a new shop or restaurant opens up near me, I make it a point to check them out. I try to make a purchase and bring someone with me whenever I can. I think that business owners need to stick together and be as supportive as we can be. Plus, it gives me a chance to check out their customer service. It's a quirky hobby, but I really learn a lot from watching people take care of others. I've noticed that a lot 'out-of-business' signs are hanging where places without any customer service used to be.

Right out of the gate, it's expensive to start a business, and it's distracting. You can get so caught up in performing tasks that your staff begins to treat the customers as an intrusion. Busy work can really get in the way of customer service. I know a place where they offer great customer service, unless they are busy. When they are busy, they feel like it's okay to rush the customers through and cut corners, and the customers should understand. Being busy is an opportunity for you to really shine in front of a large audience. If you could create an improvement with each interaction, tally it up and see how much profit that could be.

Most people think they offer great customer service and are ready to argue the fact. But I will tell you that you don't earn any extra points with your customers by covering the basics. Great customer service is more than a clean bathroom and accurate transaction.

Customers deserve more. They have too many choices these days to tolerate anything less than friendly service. Your customers deserve your very best. If they don't get it from you, they will find it somewhere else. Here's the test you can perform yourself to determine if you have extreme customer service: Does every customer brag about you or the experience? Ask your next 10 customers where they heard about you or why they choose to shop with you.

Right now, the Denver Channel is holding their A-List competition and local consumers are getting to vote for their favorite specialty store, bar or restaurant. If you look at the stats on this competition, you will notice that there are a lot of companies competing, but the number of votes between competitors is staggering. One company will have 400 votes and another will have 5. If you truly have great customer service, are your customers voting for you? Most likely, you are an expert at, or at least, you really enjoy what you've chosen to do. But that doesn't mean you have a complete plan for being a successful business owner.

Without customers, you have a really expensive hobby. With extreme customer service, you have the ability to turn each individual customer into several. Don't focus on how to drive new customers into your store, figure out how to overwhelm your current customers, and they will bring in more business for you.

I was on the phone with someone last week who runs a fitness facility. She was saying that this referral marketing doesn't really work because she has several clients who tell her, I've been trying to get my friend, sister, neighbor to join and they won't.

So for all the extreme customer service she's providing to her current customers, it's not bringing in new customers. Don't throw out good service – figure out why your customers shop with you. What are their hot buttons? What can you offer that they can't get anywhere else? Is there a risk your customers have to take to do business with you? Is there a commitment or high price tag? Is there a discomfort that they have to overcome? You have a valuable service, or you wouldn't be in business. Take some time to figure out WHY your customers shop with you, and the HOW to market to them will come.

My husband was spending a lot of time building his Facebook farm last spring. This was before he opened the doors to his own company full time. He was commenting to me one night about how great of an example the farm was a for real business owner. It teaches you to be organized, plan ahead and cover multiple tasks at once. You plant, you harvest, you sell. I had to take issue with the one detrimental flaw that seems to happen to most business owners and sales people I consult with. In the fictitious farm, you take your produce to the market and the customers come and buy it, giving you enough income to buy more seed to plant.

However, where do these customers come from? Who markets to them? How are they informed about what is available in the market place? What type of service do they receive from you? What makes them buy from your produce stand versus all the other stands out there? Are they repeat customers, or do you sell to a new set of customers every time?

This is the common struggle with most shop owners. The common belief is if they open the doors or put up an optimized website, the customers will come. But customers don't come from out of nowhere. Sometimes you'll get someone who Googled you and chose your site over someone else's. Or they happened to be walking by and liked your window display. Maybe it was the Welcome sign that lured them in, though welcome signs are extremely rare. Most storefronts are covered in "NO" or "Don't" signs, that most people have learned to ignore.

Even when I go into a new store, it's rare that my presence is welcomed in any special way. I may or may not be greeted. Most retailers don't even know how to interact with customers. They have been trained on how to use the register and how to keep the inventory looking nice, but spend hardly any time at all training their staff to talk to the customers.

One of my favorite experiences when I was in Paris was that whenever you entered a store, no matter the size, everyone greets each other. It is rude not to. And you always say goodbye and thank you before you exit. It's common sense, but it's not common practice.

In an Office Max store, my friend Nancy was treated to a great, but rare, customer experience. She had walked up to the counter and noticed the salesperson was pacing behind the registers. She asked him which register he was at, and he responded with, "whichever register you choose."

Now, we've all been the victim of this scenario at one time or another. More than once, I have found myself at the "wrong" register, because that's not where the salesperson was logged into. I've had to pick up my items and carry my stuff somewhere else so I could give the store my money. In this Office Max scenario, the store was here to provide for the customers, and at that moment, they were focusing on Nancy. She was not being treated as a transaction, but a valuable part of why Office Max is in business. This is a great example of looking through the customer's eyes.

Try being your own customer. Take a walk around your shop. Start in the parking lot and notice what your customers see. This can be a difficult exercise because you've become too familiar with your surroundings. Take your team with you, or bring on someone who is not emotionally attached. Take down the "NO" signs and the handmade notices. Instead put up professional words that welcome and thank your customers for feeding you and keeping the lights on.

Listen to the words you use with your customers and with each other. Is it full of slang like nope, yep, and sure? Are you saying yes to your customers in EVERY scenario? "Welcome to our store, I'm so glad you chose to shop with us today. How can I help you? You're just looking? Wonderful. Take your time. And make sure you notice our new display of our newest product. Everyone who tries it loves it and comes back for more. Here's a warm washcloth/ice cold water/plush seating/map of the park to make you more comfortable."

Don't share your excuses with your customers. They don't want to hear about delayed deliveries or someone else calling in sick. Handle it behind the scenes. Don't let yourself get angry or frustrated in front of a customer. If you allow yourself to get angry in that situation, how are going to handle it when something really serious happens in your life. If you're struggling with this, there's a great book out there called, Win The Customer, Not The Argument. Read it.

Take time everyday to train your team about how to treat your customers. Talk about great service and how you can duplicate it with every customer. Take the time to turn those challenging scenarios into a teachable moment. And set the standard high for your industry.

Let the economy take away the competition – and let your extreme customer service thrive and shine.

Who's In Your Passenger Seat?

In union, there is strength. - Aesop

We all want more business. We are all looking for that magic button that will create more sales and more customers just by pressing it. What we tend to overlook is the fact that we already have it. Where is it, you ask? Look at your passenger seat the next time you are headed out to an event. Is it empty or is it filled with your favorite client or that hard-to-get-to decision-maker?

With an invitation to attend a seminar, ribbon cutting or networking event, you are positioning yourself and your brand on the forefront of your client's mind. This is brilliant for re-connecting with someone when the sales trail has gone cold or you've already left several unreturned messages. When that telephone is starting to weigh in at 100 + pounds, that is your clue that it's time to invite someone along with you to the next business event you attend.

When I speak to groups about strengthening their customer ties, I get a lot of blank stares about how to accomplish this. You already know that you're supposed to follow up. You already send out a newsletter and you attend more networking events than you care to track. How does that help you meet those customers just outside of your sphere of influence?

When an airline sends an airplane off the runway, it doesn't matter whether or not that passenger seat next to you is filled or not, that airplane is headed to its destination. The airline would prefer to have all of those seats filled because it means more revenue for the company. Your vehicle is just like that airplane. A full vehicle means more revenue for your company and an empty vehicle means that only the pilot is going to benefit from this journey. Give your clients more benefit and more sales will come.

With customers, the phrase "out of sight, out of mind" really rings true. It's up to you to stay on their radar, but not to be annoying. There is a careful balance you have to pay attention to. Your clients want to hear from you. They don't want to be sold or constantly barraged with your clever sale techniques. Your customers don't want to answer questions about how close you are, on a scale from 1-10, from the closing the deal. They do want to know that they can count on you when they need you. But that might not be today. It might not be tomorrow, but their situation will change and when it does, your brand, and your brand only, needs to be on the tip of their tongue. How can you be sure that your customer thinks about you when they are ready to buy?

An invitation is the "No-Pitch Sales Pitch" that makes it really easy to pick up the phone and connect with your customers, vendors, and business associates. When you invite someone along, you add so much value to your own brand, that you don't need to even talk sales. You don't need a sales-closing statement. You don't need a gimmick. All you need is to be genuine about connecting with them. People do business with people they like and trust, but only if they remember you.

An invitation will give you multiple opportunities to call on your clients and associates, therefore training people to take your calls. If you're tired of leaving voicemails that never get returned or being snubbed by the gatekeeper, turn to the invitation-approach. Your phone calls will be welcomed. Surprise your customers with value and they will do business with you and refer others to you. Never go anywhere with your passenger seat empty, and your business will thrive in the friendly skies.

Networking Drive-By

The way of the world is meeting people through other people. – Robert Kerrigan

I'd heard about this type of networking before. It was something people made fun of, so I was sure it was a rumor, until it happened to me. I was standing with a small group of people at a networking event when suddenly, there was a business card being placed in my hand, and into the hands of those I was talking to by someone none of us knew. In a flash, this person appeared, placed his business card into stranger's hands, and disappeared. I had become the victim of a "Networking Drive-By". I don't know if you're familiar with the action, but it's not pretty. There's no warning, no introduction, just a business card flung into your hand by a speeding networker who attacks faster than a speeding bullet

When I attended my first networking event, I had no clue how to conduct myself or what the protocol was for meeting the 50+ unfamiliar faces in the room. Where do I start? How do I connect with them all?

After attending several events, I've discovered that I'm not there to meet everybody. I discovered that there is a right way and a wrong way to distribute my business card, introduce myself, and connect with the people I've met.

Nametags don't replace introductions

There is a proper way to introduce yourself in any social setting. When it comes to official networking events, often people try to skip the introduction and instead, use my name tag as a "pre" introduction. As they approach me, rather than look me in the eye, extend their hand and introduce their name, they avert their eyes to my name tag. They attempt to pronounce my business name and then ask me what I do. This always puts me on alert. Shouldn't we be introduced first? The answer is Yes.

The role of the name tag is to be a reminder to you if you've forgotten my name. But you must first learn my name. An introduction at a networking event is no different than at any other social gathering. The name tag is just a helpful reminder for you during the conversation. Do not start staring at my name tag until we've been formally introduced.

It's a networking event, not a card collecting party

I love that everyone has an automated customer management database. It's a great way to stay connected with our customers, friends, and associates. However, it seems like some people are just in the business of collecting or passing out as many cards as they can. The point of exchanging business cards is to stay connected with someone you've just met. When there is a "mutual" benefit in continuing the conversation, then exchanging business cards makes sense. When you are actually interested in their services or you want to refer them to someone else, you can exchange contact information.

If I give you my business card, I am not inviting you to add me to your automated newsletter. Always, always, ask permission to add someone to your newsletter. It is just rude to expect them to "opt-out" of something they never opted into in the first place. If you aren't comfortable asking their permission, then you need to spend more time establishing the relationship. Courtesy and customer service go together.

Take a genuine interest in others

A room full of people at a networking event does not represent a room full of potential customers to whom you can sell your wares. It does represent a room full of ambassadors. We are all ambassadors for each other. If you take the time to have a real conversation you can develop a group of people that will brag about you to others. You can learn about someone else and brag about them. When we talk about ourselves, nobody really listens. If we can get others talking about us, it is more interesting and therefore, more valuable. You are one person representing your company at an event. When you establish connections with others, they will represent you, often times, even better than you can represent yourself. The point of coming together is to learn about other businesses and share that information. Don't talk about yourself, instead, brag on someone. Make introductions. Spread the news about others. When you make people your business, people will make your business.

My friends and I all recovered quickly from our "drive-by" attack. We collected the cards and left them on the table for the one in the crowd interested in collecting as many cards as he could. For those of you with a stack of unwanted business cards, I know a child that is trying to earn his way into the Guinness Book of World Records for the most collected business cards. Send them his way. He won't add you to his newsletter.

Don't Forget To Send The Invitations

I am thankful for the mess to clean after a party because it means I have been surrounded by friends. – Nancy J Carmody

More and more, I am discovering the importance of marketing. People often share their disappointment with me over lack of attendance at seminars or other professional events. I'm often asked how to get more people to show up or how to create that buzz for their business. My answer is, don't forget to send the invitations.

When I first started my business, I felt as if I didn't know how to market. I didn't go to school for marketing and I didn't have a professional background in marketing. However, I've learned that marketing is a lot like throwing a party. I used to be a stay-at-home mom who was the hostess with the mostest when it came to throwing birthday parties and home parties. The key to a successful business shares a lot of the same guidelines as hosting a party.

Start with your guest list – this is your target market. You want to make sure that your market knows about your party, event, website or product. This is where invitations come in to play. You can have the best product or service in the world, but without customers, you have a very expensive hobby. Marketing is a lot like inviting people to your party.

Contact your guest list, not just once, but several times. First, send out a notice to save the date. When "save the date" cards first came on the scene, I thought they were a clever way for stationery places to sell twice as many invitations, but now, I love them. They allow you to build up brand recognition without selling anything. Announcing your party/business, puts your brand on your customer's brain and tongue. It gets them thinking about you and talking about you.

Sending out invitations can be done by email, Facebook, LinkedIn, Meetup.com and even the old-fashioned Post Office. But don't stop there.

Contact your guests for their confirmation. Most people don't know how to RSVP, so it's your job to find out if they're planning to attend or not. If you do this by phone, you have a great opportunity to create a conversation with your customers. I know, it's much quicker to send a blast email, which I recommend you do, too, but don't eliminate the telephone. Your voice is part of your brand. You can create a stronger connection with your customers by letting them hear your voice.

Confirm your event. A reminder email or phone call can go a long way in increased attendance. And each time you contact your guests, you put your brand in front of them. You get to answer questions, maybe even schedule an appointment or make a sale.

After your party, thank your guests for coming by sending them a handwritten thank you card. And for those guests who couldn't make it, they should get a card, too, letting them know they were missed.

Don't throw a party without sending out the invitations. And don't worry if you don't have a marketing background; you can hire a professional. Spend more time marketing for your business than you do planning the party, and you'll be a success.

Getting Past The Gatekeeper

I am the Gatekeeper! – Dana Barrett

I was at the bookstore today and grabbed a book off the shelf titled "Get More Referrals" or something similar in that genre of titles. I opened to the middle – which is typical behavior for me in determining whether or not I like the book – and read a section titled "getting past the gatekeeper".

Getting past the gatekeeper is one of those topics that every sales person is still trying to master. There are books, articles and seminars all over discussing this one roadblock to making sales. So, what is the master secret to getting past the gatekeeper?

I read through the author's script of how to answer the questions that are always asked, such as "What company are you with?" in varying degrees of semantics. What I read irritated me to the point of slamming the book closed and deciding to leave the bookstore all together. They did not have what I wanted, and now I was irritated at the information my own customers are bombarded with when they go looking for answers.

The author talked about creating a false sense of familiarity with the person on the phone, or the company, or the person they are trying to reach. UGH! My thoughts were steaming as I wondered (out loud) to myself – Who really gets away with this?

At some point, your cards are unveiled and your charade is discovered. Even IF these tactics work, you are bluffing your way in, and the recipient of your bluff knows it. Only now, you've lost any possible credibility you might have had if you earned the phone call honestly. As you're talking, aren't you now facing an uphill battle because everything you say now has to go through a filter of "if you bluffed there, where else will you be bluffing?" Can you be viewed as credible? Can your sales pitch be trusted? If you weren't honest from the beginning, then how do I know you aren't going to continue to lie to me?

Here is how you get past the gatekeeper: Ask somebody you already know to make an introduction to the decision maker. Most likely, between your Friends, Relatives, Associates, Neighbors and Customers, you have a connection to every potential customer you would like to meet. When you are introduced by a mutual acquaintance, the likeliness of closing the deal is greatly increased, especially if you have something to truly offer. Strengthen those relationships and they will help introduce you to the right people.

Don't play charades and do something that "sounds like" familiarity. Go out and actually create it. That sounds like a closed deal.

SURE-Fire Extreme Customer Service

*Quality in a service or product is not what you put into it.
It is what the client or customer gets out of it.* – Peter Drucker

Zig Ziglar says, "You can have everything in life that you want if you will just help enough other people get what they want."

What do you want? Isn't that a fundamental question that we, as service industry professionals, ask our customers on a daily basis? Is that not the question that drives the entity that we call, "business"?

In 1976, American restaurant Burger King developed an advertising slogan: "Have it Your Way". That slogan came with a nifty little jingle that many of us can bring to memory without my even having to print the words here. Burger King executives took a monumental step with this advertising campaign by bypassing the question altogether, and simply offering the answer that every customer was looking for.

All too often, we in the business world seem to forget the question, and wonder in retrospect why it is so difficult to offer our customers an answer. And so the purpose of this article is to bring us back to the basics when it comes to customer service. From there, I will share with you our system of "Extreme Customer Service" that will catapult your return on investment with each and every one of your current and potential customers.

Fundamental #1 – Everyone Wants Something

You want something. Your customer wants something. We all have wants, and a fundamental value of doing business is to discover what it is your customer wants – and then find a way to provide that to him or her. If we are to believe business guru, Zig Ziglar, then all we have to do is help enough people attain what they want, and our wants will materialize in turn. I actually believe this. But I also think we need to expound upon the concept just a little bit.

On the surface, it would seem obvious; maybe even easy, to discover what it is our customers want. But if one is to objectively look at the service industry as a whole, it becomes apparent that there are those who get the concept – and a myriad of those who think they get it, but are failing miserably in their practical application.

Those who get it seem to have a deeper understanding of what it is the customer "really" wants. A loan officer at a bank will do well to understand that what their customer wants is NOT money, but the ability to translate the money into their dream. Be it a new home, or a remodeling project, or that new car or a vacation – these are all deeply connected to the self-esteem of the customer, and therefore are the real assets being applied for when asking for the loan to make the dreams come true.

The insurance agent who believes that what they are selling is just an auto policy to enable their customer to comply with the basics of the law, misses out on the fact that what they have to offer their customer is peace of mind should the unthinkable happen.

Fundamental #2 – Everyone Has Something to Offer

All too often, I think that people in business find themselves in the wrong line of work because they have focused their attention upon whatever the latest fad says is popular. In 1987, there were virtually no independent specialty coffee shops here in America. Then along came a man named Howard Schultz who translated his passion for connecting with people, and excellent coffee into a $9.41 billion business. The name of that business is synonymous with coffee, worldwide. By the mid 1990's, people realized what a huge industry coffee had become, and we started seeing independent coffee houses open up on virtually every corner in America.

Coffee shops come and go with great regularity. And in so many instances, when an independent shop closes its doors, the chief complaint offered by the owners is, "no one can compete against such a giant as Starbucks." But I suggest that the issue that drives more business out of business isn't so much about overwhelming competition – but about misplaced priorities and a backward model of what makes a business successful in the first place.

In Fortune Magazine, Howard Schultz says, "We aren't in the coffee business serving people; we are in the people business serving coffee." Herein lies one key to the success Starbucks has seen over the last 21 years. Schultz started with his combined passions, people and coffee, and did what came naturally.

So many times, it seem that business people start with the business – even if it is a business that they know nothing about – and do whatever they can to run it just like the other guys. If you are missing the key ingredient – your passion – then I believe that you are on the fast track to business extinction.

Find what you are really good at. Discover what you really love. Translate your talent or gift into a business model that is a natural extension of yourself – and you will be surprised to discover that there are people (your customers) who share the same passions, and who will pay a premium to purchase your services.

In the 1989 movie, "Field of Dreams", the character played by Kevin Costner was a rural farmer who hears a mysterious voice tell him, "If you build it, he will come". The character in the movie imagines building a baseball diamond in his cornfield, and despite skepticism and disbelieving hecklers, eventually sees his passion for a connection with his father, who loved the game of baseball, turned into reality.

Our System of Extreme Customer Service

Let's assume that you have discovered what your true passion is, and have translated that passion into a business model that caters to those customers who share your interests. You are helping others get what they want, and in turn, they are helping you get what you want. Extreme customer service demands that you not only meet the needs of your customers, but that you exceed them.

Michael Port, in his book, Book Yourself Solid, says, "give away so much value that you think you've given too much and then give more."

Our system requires a fresh look, outside the normal parameters of how business is done to delineate what it looks like to exceed your customer's expectations. One should never look at a sale as a "transaction", but instead as an opportunity to answer our customer's question without it ever having to be asked.

If you are in the retail industry and make it a priority to greet every customer who comes into your place if business, then your greeting should be sincere and open-ended. Don't just ask, "how are you" with the expectation of a simple "fine" for an answer. Rather, truly inquire as to the well being of your customer. Such action requires a paradigm shift in the way we think of our customers. They do not represent "transactions", but relationships.

And if you are to treat each customer as though their relationship is important to you, it stands to reason that you will, over the course of time, get to know them. In that discovery process, you will learn of their likes and dislikes. You will learn of their family life and about the activities in which they, or members of their family are involved. These discoveries then translate into your being better equipped to anticipate your customer's wants and needs – and you are well on way to extreme customer service in action.

Earlier in this article, I mentioned your return on investment as it relates to your current and potential customers. Anyone in business can appreciate the risk involved in building and developing a successful business model. There are tangible and intangible elements of investment, and some weigh heavier than others. And given the notion that we are to treat our customers as though they were relationships worthy of development – there is a corresponding element of risk that is associated with the investment here as well.

May I close this article with this suggestion: Investing in your customers – taking the time to care enough to get to know them... anticipating their wants and exceeding their expectations... is always worth the investment. As with any relationship, there is an element of vulnerability that necessarily accompanies such an emphasis upon the humanity of our business. But without the people who are our customers – we would not be in business at all.

Invest In People

What I am interested in is investing in people. – Arthur Rock

As this article is being written, the Bureau of Economic Research has declared the United States is "officially" in a recession. This announcement comes as no surprise to economists and consumers in general. All of us are aware of the challenging economy, and all of us have been touched, or know someone who has been touched by this market. Commentary abounds on how to get through these difficult times... Tighten the belt. Eliminate excessive spending. Cut the workforce. The list goes on and on.

Everyone has an opinion... and I suppose that I am no different. And so with that in mind, may I offer my opinion, and support it with two or three proofs that will justify your consideration?

At least one thing in business is fundamental: Without customers, you do not have a "business" – you have an expensive hobby. Here's another: Your customers are people – and all people have needs. Find the way to meet those needs, in an overwhelmingly satisfying way, and you will recession-proof your business. How do you do that? Invest in your people.

People are your business' most valuable resource. They hold irreplaceable value. As such, they require every consideration and considerable investment in order to ride out a "down" economy. Rather than tightening, eliminating and cutting... consider investing – perhaps even sacrificially so.

We invest in what we value. It would be ridiculous to consider pouring resources into something that would bear out no return on your investment (ROI). It is an established fact that the cost of generating new customers is upwards of ten times those of nurturing your existing customer base. And why would you consider investing in your existing customer base? Because it is from that very source that you will generate a loyal fan base that will in turn generate referrals, thereby filling your pipeline with much needed revenue.

How then, shall you go about the process of investing in your customers? There are endless ways. Let's explore just a few.

Hold an Event

On a monthly basis, host some type of an event that honors your top customers. A dinner party... a cocktail party... an award or recognition ceremony. This is not a time to "sell" your business. This is a time to build relationships.

The value to holding such events is played out in the deepening of ties between you and those who have already supported you and your business. These are the people upon whose lips you want your company's name at all times.

When they need you again, or when they are speaking with someone who needs your services... you are the one they will remember.

Give a Gift

Everyone loves receiving gifts. And gift-giving doesn't have to be "mushy". But on-target gift-giving requires forethought and consideration. In short, the gift must be relevant to the recipient. If you know that your customer collects sports memorabilia – then when they're not expecting it (and especially when it's not associated in any way to any type of a "sell") – bring them some small item that acknowledges their passion for things athletic.

If you know that they love coffee – bring them a pound of beans, or a coffee cup, or a flavored syrup that you know they'll enjoy. How do you discover what their "thing" is?? As you develop your relationship with them, these tidbits of trivia will come to the surface during conversations. How do you make sure trivia is not "trivial"? You remember the details – and then implement them into your interactions with them. What's the point? You are the one they will remember.

Tell Someone Else about Them

Want to go the extra mile with your customers? Discover what line of business they are in, and find someone who needs their service or product... and make an introduction. Want to start an irreversible flow of goodwill and the subsequent increase to your own business' bottom line? Do it again. And again. And again. Become known as the guy (or gal) who helps your customers by bringing them more business... and guess what? You are the one that they will remember!

Too hokey for you? Think it won't work? Run a simple little test: Intentionally smile at 10 people in the next hour, and record with a single word their reaction. Did they smile back? Did they frown? Were they confused? Were they surprised? Take the 10 reactions and separate them into 2 columns – positive and negative. I'd be willing to bet that most people will see 80% or higher end up in the positive column. Why? People return kindness for kindness. If you smile at me – I am nearly certain to smile back at you. I may not know why. I may wonder what you're up to. But there's just something about being nice to people, that evokes an in-kind response in most cases.

Extrapolate this truth to investing in your customers, and you will start a chain-reaction of goodwill within your customer relationships that will absolutely yield a positive net gain in your business' bottom line. The upside is huge, and the risk is nil. Investing doesn't require significant amounts of money. It simply requires a strategic plan of action starting with knowing in what (or whom) you are investing.

Invest in your people, and watch your business grow – regardless of what the economy is doing.

One Campaign Leads To Another

Even a minor event in the life of a child is an event of that child's world, and thus a world event. – Gaston Bachelard

If you hang around Angel or me for very long, you are guaranteed to hear about our passion for campaigns as an effective alternative method of business development. A campaign is defined as an event or promotion – or just something worthy of getting the word out – and is often associated with multiple methods of connecting with your existing customer base.

Our friend in business owns a trailer shop in Englewood, CO. He recently ran a campaign (a pig roast) that was designed to honor his existing customers. It was a huge success. Whereas he was expecting a turnout of about 35-40 people, more than twice that many showed up. He honored his "best" customer with a beautifully framed photo, commemorating the great relationship that they share. He aligned with several other companies, and promoted their work as well as his own. And he touched the lives of many in the process.

Today, that man is already planning his next campaign. And as we sat across the table discussing it, one thing became clear: one campaign really does lead to another. His first campaign led to this next one. This next one will actually require several sub-campaigns... each one designed to do one thing: connect the business owner with his audience.

And therein lies the key to our passion for campaigns! It doesn't matter what business you're in... You are in the relationship business! Connecting with your existing customer base – with no intention of selling them anything is quite possibly one of the best things you could do as a business owner! They've already purchased from you – and the assumption is that you did a great job for them. But extreme customer service starts AFTER the sale. When you already made that transaction – and STILL are interested in developing that relationship – you become very valuable to them – and they to you.

Whether it's a grand re-opening, or the announcement of your newest employee... try developing a campaign around the news – and touch your customers by inviting them to share in the celebration! Find several ways to reconnect with your customers, and you just might be surprised... they might find new ways to reconnect with you! People do business with people they know, like and trust. A campaign is a great way to keep your brand on the tips of their tongues so that the next time they, or someone they know need(s) your service or product – YOU will be the one they think of!

But business owner beware: one campaign does in fact lead to another... and those campaigns and their subsequent touches inevitably lead to the success of your business! Buckle up... Great things ahead!

Your Customer – Friend or Foe?

*Don't be yourself. Be someone
a little nicer. – Mignon McLaughlin*

I was sitting on an airplane when my son woke up next to me. He had slept through the beverage service so I asked to trade in my unopened can of club soda for a lemon-lime soda for him. When I handed back my can to the flight attendant, she looked at it and told me that she would have to throw the can away.

I was perplexed by the thought of throwing away a perfectly untouched can of soda until I realized that it was a necessary safety precaution. What if I had tampered with the can before returning it to her? With our country's security at stake, it's better for the airlines to be safe than sorry.

Though, the airlines aren't the only industry treating their customers like suspects. My bank has a sign asking me to remove my sunglasses upon entering their building. I see customer policies everywhere that are policing every customer move. It got me thinking about customer service. If you are constantly worried about the threat that your customer is to you, can you offer great customer service at the same time?

Offering great customer service is all about being friendly and helpful. It's about taking care of the people that make your business run. Protecting your business from shoplifters and criminal acts is all about fear, security and policies. When you train your employees, do you concentrate more on fear or friendliness? Your business thrives on customers, yet, where do you invest the most time: discussing mandated customer policies or training creative ways to exceed your customer's expectations?

As a shop owner or bank teller, you are trained to watch every customer for signs that they are a potential thief or burglar. You've installed two-way mirrors, surveillance cameras, and tough policies. Instead of focusing on great customer service, you've implemented security practices that fuel the fear of being taken advantage of.

Unless you are filling your company handbooks with great principles on how to exceed your customer's expectations, how can you truly offer excellent customer service?

Take a look at your business through your customer's eyes. How often are you treating your customer as the enemy? How often do you get your customer to smile or say "Wow"? Do you answer the phone with a generic greeting, or do you practice saying something creative that makes your customer feel glad he called? When you're protecting your business against the feared destructive behavior of your customers, you are hindering your employees from offering genuine help. When you come up with creative ways to turn ordinary events into extreme customer service, your customers get a chance to talk about you.

Rather than think of your customer as the enemy, consider what you can do to turn them into a customer for life. Consider adopting this motto: Our company policy is to exceed your expectations.

There are practices that have snuck their way in to your business that maybe you haven't realized are sending a negative message to your customers.

I was at a bank trying to make a cash deposit when the teller wrote across my bill with a special marker, then she ran it under an ultra-violet light, looked up the serial number in a binder and then went across the bank to show the bill to another employee. All the while, I'm left standing, waiting with no explanation. I watched as she was trying to prove that I was guilty of depositing a counterfeit bill. The bill was not counterfeit. As a customer, is it important for me to watch this process?

Consider the negative effects your practices have on your customers. Everyday, we tell our customers "NO" in such subtle ways as not offering a public bathroom, unanswered phone calls, cluttered countertops and not being friendly. How difficult do you make it for your customers to do business with you?

As a customer, my every move is watched by surveillance cameras, my money is crosschecked for signs of fraud, I am considered suspicious and yet, I'm supposed to feel welcomed and served. Right now, it's easy to blame low sales on economics, but does your lack of customer service play a bigger role than you are considering? Are you impressing your customers so much that they can't help but talk about you?

Sadly, the effects of 9/11 are very real. So are counterfeiting and shoplifting. Does this mean that the airlines and banks can never offer great customer service? Are they doomed by their circumstances? Is there a way to protect your business while making your customers feel valued?

It's not rocket science - it's people science.

Smile. Be friendly. Spend time in a conversation and you will be surprised at how often your customer will tell you what they truly want from you. Look for ways to actually help your customer. They may not be spending a lot of money right now, so this is the time to strengthen their opinion of you. Give them something memorable to talk about. If you overwhelm them with service and create a memory, they will share your business with their friends and coworkers.

There are certain aspects of your business that you need to protect from your customers. You ensure that your customer never sees your trash because it doesn't provide the right impression. It smells and it looks bad. The same goes for policies that don't ensure great customer service. If your customers don't receive value in seeing it, don't show it to them. Rather than having the surveillance monitors in front for your customers to see, put them in the back room out of sight. If you have to crosscheck cash, do it discreetly under the counter. If you have to throw something away for fear of tampering, take it behind the scenes.

Consider your business as your stage and put on a performance that will call for an encore. Make sure the experience your customer has is one worth sharing.

If your customers aren't sharing your story or coming back, they may just be shopping around. Protecting your business is important. Protecting your customers is far more valuable.

What To Do If The Sky Is Falling

A piece of the sky? Shaped like a stop sign?
Not again! – Chicken Little

Unless you live in a cave, under a rock and you haven't upgraded your analog television set since 1983 – you are probably aware of the very difficult economic situation that is affecting all of us in business. Many people, perhaps even you, have been laid off, let go or are facing the very real possibility of such a reality in the near future. So what do you do, when it feels like the sky is falling? Here are a few suggestions that Experience Pros offers to our clients in the course of their consultations:

Go Proactive

We're talking about the difference between a thermometer, and a thermostat. A thermometer reacts to the temperature. A thermostat tells the temperature what it should be. The natural tendency in response to tough times is to "react". It's human nature. But we suggest that rather than reacting, you take the lemons of life and proactively make lemonade.

Grieve for a moment if you must, but it is essential to your future success that you get up, and get going in a forward direction. No one is going to do it for you... you must have a plan, and then act upon that plan until your circumstance changes for the better. Below, we'll outline a very practical plan of action for you to follow if you discover that your sky has threatened to fall.

Cover your assets – Now is the time to update your resume, listing all of your most current and/or target specific skills. You may require more than one resume, depending upon the market you want to pursue. Professional staffing services provide a full compliment of business coaching services that will literally propel you to the top of the class when it comes to writing a cover letter, a resume, or honing your interview skills to give you the competitive advantage over the masses of people all looking for jobs today. If you're serious about finding a new job – hiring a professional team to get you ready provides your "ace in the hole"!

Take a number and get online – Run, don't walk to find the number of someone who specializes in technical consultation and training. They will absolutely position you and your job search in the right places where you can be seen, noticed, and who knows... maybe even hired! The business culture is changing at the speed of WWW, and a technical consultant can help you understand the value of leveraging social networks such as LinkedIn, Meetup and Facebook to actually work for you in your job search.

Do business after hours – It's not so much what you know... as who knows you. And the very best way to make sure that the right people know you, is to put yourself where they congregate. If you are a part of a chamber of commerce or trade association, now is not the time to quit attending their networking functions. Now is the time to throw yourself full into them! There are many groups and events that are part of how Chambers of Commerce and professional trade associations offer valuable opportunities to members to connect with other members. Be intentional about whom you want to meet. Work with a marketing and visibility consultant to arrange introductions. And above all else – follow up with those people you encounter!

It's true. Times are difficult. You might even actually believe that the sky is falling. The question isn't whether or not life's dealt you a difficult hand. The question is: what are you going to do about it? Action is almost always better than non-action. Go proactive, and tell the temperature what it should be today!

Pretty Isn't Always Pink

*Things are pretty, graceful, rich, elegant, handsome...
But until they speak to the imagination,
not yet beautiful.* – Ralph Waldo Emerson

Each day we are targeted by advertisements, marketing campaigns and solicitations. From the moment we open our eyes, we have 3000-4000 chances to make a buying decision. How do we filter through the chaos? I've created my own filtering process to help make many of these decisions. It turns out that many of the designers on staff for the magazine, Metropolitan Home, use this same filtering process. They say to only surround yourself with things your find to be useful or beautiful. I'm not talking about flash over substance. I say, that when useful and beautiful come together, you have pretty.

Have you ever found that a new way of thinking may lead you into something completely different from what you originally envisioned – but often more rewarding? Can wanting something to be pretty be a fresh way of deciding whether or not to surround myself with particular items?

I like my surroundings to be clear of clutter, but it's an uphill battle. I've come to find that my world is so easily cluttered. I find myself in a perpetual state of filtering. If I can create a mental system where everything surrounding me must fit through my pretty-filter, I can create my own utopia. I want my world to be productive, clean, inspiring. I don't want to create unnecessary waste. In fact, green may even be the new pink. Reducing our carbon footprint is pretty. Planting a tree, walking, and cleaning up the neighborhood trails are pretty efforts for the environment and for our souls. Doing something to take care of yourself is pretty. Always doing something selfish is not pretty. Creating a better tomorrow is pretty. Leaving a mess for someone else to clean up is not pretty. Laughing out loud and living in the moment is pretty. Receiving extreme customer service is pretty. Being in a conversation where someone never looks me in the eye is not pretty. Getting a bargain and having my phone calls returned is pretty. Leaving inept phone messages is not pretty.

Pretty goes beyond pink. It goes beyond matching. Pretty means that the packaging or the jargon you are using to get me to make a purchase does not confuse me. Pretty means that it doesn't take away from who I am, but rather, adds to improve my situation or myself.

Pretty is with purpose. Pretty is practical. Pretty has a bit of luxury thrown in. Often, what starts out as luxury can quickly become an essential item. If we find it to be useful, we will spend more for it; our laptop computers, cell phones, navigational systems, eye-lasik surgery and more have found their way into our essential life.

Recently, I purchased a case to carry around my laptop computer. I think that my sleek computer is pretty with its silver case and apple icon that glows when it's turned on. But, carrying it around in a boring black leather bag just didn't suit me. At least, I didn't know that it didn't suit me until I saw the pretty but practical laptop case that spoke to me from my eye-level on the shelf. I respect clever marketing when I see it and when I read the tag quoting that it was pretty on the outside, and practical on the inside, I knew this bag was for me. How smart. With extra pockets and a shoulder strap – it was practical. And being practical made it even prettier to me.

Stacy London, from The Learning Channel's "What Not to Wear" says that there is something emotionally rewarding about looking good. It makes you feel more confident. It's a means of self-expression and a great tool in building self-esteem. What better marketing tool do we have than self-expression and confidence? What's prettier than that?

Help me create an experience that doesn't drive me into debt, buyer's remorse or confusion over what you just sold to me. That's not pretty. I want to feel good. I want to experience an emotional reaction from within. I want to provide additional quality to my life. If I'm going to add to the clutter of my life, or to the clutter of my client's life, shouldn't it add value? If your product or service isn't attractive, why would I take a second glance? Enrich my life and I'll feel pretty. Won't you?

Business Etiquette

Email Etiquette

We've got email going out. We've got newsletters going out. We're just trying to keep them informed. – Kevin Hamilton

Using email etiquette increases your chances of your correspondence being opened and read. A lot of people don't bother to read an email before they send it out, as proven from the many spelling and grammar mistakes contained in so many emails. Instill some email etiquette and protocol, then read through your email through the eyes of the recipient. This will help you send more effective messages and avoid misunderstandings and inappropriate comments.

Email Etiquette

Every email should have all your contact information (full name, title, logo, address, phone, email, fax). If your email is forwarded or printed out, you want to be sure your contact information follows the paper trail, or e-paper trail. If you send something worthwhile, the hope is that your message will be forwarded. Make sure people can contact you.

The cc: field is to be used sparingly. It's confusing to most people. When you put someone's name in the cc: field, it means that you want them to be aware of the information, but you aren't expecting them to respond. Though, recipients might not know who is supposed to act on the message. When responding to a cc: message, include the other recipient in the cc: field as well because they've already been brought into the conversation and confusion abounds if you leave them out now.

Include the original message thread included in your reply email. There are too many details being shared via email and to make sure everyone knows what you're responding to, you have to include the original notes. This saves everyone frustration from having to search out previously related emails for the information.

Quickly respond. Customers send an email because they wish to receive a quick response. If they don't get a quick response from you, they will most likely contact your competitor. Each email should be replied to within twenty-four hours, and preferably within the same working day. If the email is complicated, quickly send an email back saying that you have received it and that you will get back to them. This will put the customer's mind at rest and usually customers will then be very patient with you.

Use proper spelling, grammar and punctuation. Improper spelling and grammar gives your company a bad image. Your program has a spell-check function. You can turn it on to automatically spell check your emails before sending. This minor inconvenience will no doubt save you from embarrassment down the road.

Each email should focus on a single topic. If you have to discuss several topics, send multiple emails, each with their own subject line so each person can recall the information later. Use short paragraphs and short sentences to make it easier for the recipient to read.

Templates are a real time saver for repeated information such a directions and how-to enroll in your seminars. This ensures a consistent customer experience and saves you time when you save the text is a word document or a pre-formatted email.

The To: field is not the field to use when sending an email mailing. Some people place all the email addresses in this field but there are two downsides to this practice: (1) the recipient knows that you have sent the same message to a large number of recipients, and it's not personal, and (2) you are publicizing someone's email address without their permission. One way to get round this is to place all addresses in the Bcc: field. However, the recipient will only see the address from the To: field in their email, so if this was empty, the To: field will be blank and this might look like spamming. You could include the mailing list email address in the To: field, or even better, if you have Microsoft Outlook and Word you can do a mail merge and create one message for each recipient. A mail merge also allows you to use fields in the message so that you can address each recipient personally. For more information on how to do a Word mail merge, consult the Help in Word.

End your email with a link to your website. Your email signature can offer a link to something of interest or value to the recipient. Once there, have a call-to-action that brings them further into your sales process.

Email is a great way to answer questions and to anticipate further questions. If you do not answer all the questions in the original email, you will receive further emails regarding the unanswered questions, which will not only waste your time and your customer's time but also cause considerable frustration. Moreover, if you are able to anticipate relevant questions, your customer will be grateful and impressed with your efficient and thoughtful customer service. Imagine for instance that a customer sends you an email asking which credit cards you accept. Instead of just listing the credit card types, you can guess that their next question will be about how they can order, so you also include some order information and a link to your order page. Your customers will appreciate this.

Email can be a powerful relationship building tool to connect with your customers, if it's used in a genuine way. Attempt to make your emails as personal as possible. Use the active voice of a verb wherever possible. For instance, 'We will process your order today', sounds better than 'Your order will be processed today'. The first sounds more personal, and email has the tendency to take on an impersonal and unnecessarily formal tone.

RSVP Etiquette Will Grow Your Business

People don't RSVP because they're hedging their bets. They leave it up to you to call them, and sometimes they still won't give you an answer. – Michael Bassett

Often times, you are invited to an event and the first thing you think of is "what's in it for me?" You decide by the title if the event is going to be worthwhile or not. Furthermore, you're unsure of the etiquette of RSVP'ing. Do you RSVP if you ARE going to attend? Or, do you RSVP if you AREN'T planning to attend? Different hosts ask for different responses, which add to further confusion.

What is the proper way to RSVP and how does this affect the growth of your business? Recently, several Chambers of Commerce have moved their events & programs onto Meetup.com to help solve both of these struggles. In an effort to help gain more awareness and more attendance at their events, they've incorporated Meetup.com to help you out.

Meetup.com asks for a YES or a NO response right away and allows you to view who is planning to attend, to rate the events and even post your profile. It's a great tool to bring more people together. Your profile serves as 'google food', which means it helps out with your search engine optimization. This is all great for growing your business, however, the RSVP question still lingers.

As business professionals, you are really busy trying to wear many hats – while juggling a full calendar. If you RSVP too early, then you feel like you are too committed, but if you RSVP too late, the host may feel like they should cancel the event, even though there are probably a lot of people interested in attending.

So, here's how to RSVP properly and grow your business at the same time; take 2 minutes to read about the event as soon as you receive the announcement. Do it right away and you can clear this 'to-do' off of your list. Compare it to your calendar. If you are available, say YES and think of someone to invite along. If you aren't available, encourage someone else to go. After all, this is your chamber, and you add value when you show up, support the host, the event, and the others in attendance. Your business will increase, your chamber membership is strengthened, and you'll be a success.

RSVP today.

The Etiquette of Networking

The test of good manners if to be patient with bad ones. - Gabirol

Everyday we are out meeting people, but how many of us really know the etiquette of networking? Is networking different than meeting people? It must be because when I attend a networking event, all social manners seem to disappear from the people who try to meet me.

Tell me if you can relate to this, you are at a networking event and someone comes up to you and instead of extending their hand and introducing themselves, they avert their eyes to your chest and attempt to read your name tag. Because I have a tricky name, they always mispronounce my name and my company name.

Since when did it become acceptable to skip the introduction?

Networking Etiquette

There are lots of blogs about having an introduction speech and bringing business cards and doing your homework about the people you are hoping to meet. I'm talking about the etiquette of networking; how to introduce yourself, where to place your name tag, RSVPing and saying thank you.

Introduce Yourself

At a networking event, or anytime you meet someone new, introduce yourself. Extend your right hand, look them into the eyes, smile and say "Hi, my name is...." If the receiver is courteous, they will respond with the same gesture and the response of "It's nice to meet you (name), my name is...

Nametag

Wear your nametag on your right lapel, not on a lanyard that falls at your belly. When your name tag is located on your right lapel, the receiver can read your name and hear the correct pronunciation at the same time allowing them to further commit it to memory. They can also use the name tag as a refresher later in the conversation.

Don't Rush

Take your time when you meet someone new to ask qualifying questions that help you get to know them better. Will they be a friend, a potential customer or someone in your network? Not everyone you meet is a potential customer, so taking the time at the introduction will help you decide how to categorize them into your database. Knowing who your target market is will help you with categorizing. Consider this to be a time of discovery. Ask yourself, how can I help this person?

Talk With People You Already Know

I know several people who feel like they aren't productive at a networking event unless they meet a certain number of new people. I suggest spending time with people you already know and add new people to the conversation as they walk by. This allows you to brag about the person you already know. It puts everyone at ease because you aren't standing with a group of strangers wondering what to say first. Make introductions all around the group every time someone new enters the circle.

Take The Time To Remember Names

This isn't foolproof so I have a back up plan. My friends and I have a signal that we use in case we run into someone familiar at another event. If this has happened to you, I apologize. If we meet someone at the mall, or anywhere around town, if I don't immediately make the introduction, my friends know that I've forgotten their name. They will extend their hand and tell them their own name. The courteous will reply their name back and now nobody has to feel awkward.

Keep Your Business Cards In Your Pocket

The only proper time to exchange business cards is if there is a mutually beneficial reason to. When I hand you my business card, I am not signing up for your newsletter. While most people see a networking event as a place to hand out and receive 50 business cards, it isn't. It's a great place to connect with people, build your social network and create brand recognition for your business.

This is a place to create trust and credibility. This is a place to refer other businesses, not to close sales or make deals. Those who are the best at networking are there to create relationships. They gain admirers and strong connections of people who will take their phone calls and answer their emails. Their friendliness extends to everyone.

Always Let The Hosts Know Whether Or Not You Are Coming

It is rude to not to announce your plans in advance. If you truly don't know if you will be able to attend or not, let the host know and make a commitment you can stick to. Catering is almost always paid for in advance, so your attendance is counted on in someone else's wallet.

Say Thank You

Afterwards, thank the hosts for the gathering. Say nice things about the event, whether or not you found it difficult or easy to meet people. If they ran out of food, it's probably because not enough people responded. If it was difficult to join conversations, consider whether or not your own motives were only to pass out cards or to really connect with people.

Follow Up

If you exchanged business cards with anyone, follow up immediately. Don't wait for the other person to do it. They may not have read my blog.

Business By The Numbers

5 Ways To Drive Customer Loyalty

An ounce of loyalty is worth a pound of cleverness – Elbert Green Hubbard

Once you've earned your customer's attention and the sale, your real work begins. According to surveys, customer satisfaction is at an all time high, while customer loyalty is at an all time low. Gaining new customers isn't nearly as challenging for companies as developing loyal customers. Yet, there are 5 top things you can start today that drive customer loyalty.

Customer's emotions have real financial implications for business. Emotion will drive your customer to dump their current brand and come looking for yours. A lot of new business comes to you because a customer was dissatisfied with how they were being treated by your competition.

Reward Your Current Customers

When you shop at Kohl's, Michaels or Bath & Body Works, you are given a "Repeat Receipt". A "Repeat Receipt" offers a great discount if you return to the store within a short amount of time. They reward the customers who are already in their stores; the customers who are already buying from them and who already trust them for business. One of Starbucks' most effective campaigns is their "treat receipt" special that gets you to return THE VERY SAME DAY for a second purchase. This one campaign dramatically increases sales, and has subsequently seen multiple replays in their retail stores nationwide.

Fun And Games

Newspapers, magazines and online media know that when you involve user-participation, people will always come back for more. Playing games and solving puzzles is a sought-out leisure activity. Corporate websites that draw customers in with interaction and fun activities are the most talked about and blogged about sites of all. Millions of people visit websites every day, and you can connect with your customers by making better use of your corporate website.

Stop Policing Your Customers

Incorporate policies that encourage your customers. Encouraged customers will share the brands they love with others. Eliminate policies that hurt your customers. Do more of things that keep your customers happy. Do fewer things that irritate them. This is not rocket-science… it's people-science!

Take Care Of Every Single Customer

Each department should be in sync with a unified goal: Take care of every single customer. Period. Whether they bought online, in your store or from another department, take care of the customer. In Don Gallegos' book, he talks about an angry customer returning a gallon of milk to their grocery store. His team was trained to give a full refund with no questions asked. If the customer was dissatisfied, this store took care of it.

Simple. Even though the gallon of milk had the label from a competing store, his store still took care of the customer, and earned a lifetime of loyalty.

Be Nice To Angry Customers

At some point, you will discover that you cannot please every one of your customers all of the time. They might get angry... but they are still your customers. The more prepared you are for it, the better the outcome will be for both you and your customer. An angry customer provides an opportunity to really show what your brand is made of.

Your Customers Will Only Be As Loyal As You Are.

It is worth the extra time and resources to turn a SINGLE unsatisfied customer into a satisfied one. Author Pete Blackshaw says it's cheap insurance to pay off a refund, rather than find yourself as the YouTube video generating thousands of negative views a day. Customers who are engaged with positive, authentic experiences, will share their experience with others and come back for more.

Emotion is everything. American poet Maya Angelou says, "I've learned that people will forget what you said, people will forget what you did, but people will never forget how you made them feel." You can create brand-loyalty by meeting your customers' emotional needs.

3 Ways To Stay In Touch

If I had a single flower for every time I think about you, I could walk forever in my garden. – Claudia Ghandi

Staying in touch with your past customers is a proven way to keep your customers thinking about you. In essence, when your customers hear from you, they are reminded of you. They start thinking about you again. When they are thinking about you, they are more likely to conduct business with you and refer you to other people they know.

Rather than sending out impersonal mail or a sales flyer with a coupon, create a system for staying in touch on a regular basis that is easy, repeatable and practical. When your system is simple, you're more likely to stick with it. Your consistency is key for staying in touch with past customers.

Invite, Introduce and share Interests with your customers

Invitations – Invite your customers to events you are attending or holding. Look at your address book and choose four events each year to invite your customers to. An invitation makes people feel special and offers a great reminder of your brand to your customers.

Introductions – Introduce people to each other who would never have met naturally. Invite 3-5 people to join you for coffee each week. Look for something in common and make introductions. An introduction can add value to their lives and it reminds your customers of you.

Interests – Send articles, links, or book ideas to your customers. Seek out books or articles that you think they might be interested. This step requires that you know something about your customers. These interests can point back to your industry, but it's not necessary. The re-connection with you is often enough of a touch to keep your customers thinking about you.

Inviting, introducing and sharing interests will keep your brand on the tip of your customer's tongue. Creating customer conversation is the most perfect form of marketing and you can create that conversation by staying in touch with your customers.

10 Ways To Boost Your Energy

Energy and persistence conquer all things – Benjamin Franklin

Great customer service depends not only on your ability to offer friendly service, it also requires a bit of energy on your part. What do you do when the afternoon slump is begging you for a nap or that early morning meeting starts before your cup of coffee kicks in?

When you boost your energy level, even momentarily, you increase your happiness quotient, reduce stress and improve your overall health by boosting your immunity. You will also offer better customer service than your competition. When you boost your energy, you'll boost your level of service.

Here are 10 tips to boost your energy level

1. Move it. Try not to schedule meetings right after lunch. Your body is digesting and the temptation to nod off is strongest. Rather, use this time to for those tasks that require some physical fitness: put inventory away, re-arrange furniture, and walk files over to your co-workers. Filing, sorting, and stocking are great activities to re-energize you.

2. Play your favorite song. Often, just hearing the first opening bars will get you humming and offer you a momentary surge of energy that will reduce stress and the feeling of fatigue. Fun music is also proven to increase sales because customers who feel good are more likely to spend more. Do you remember how excited you got making a mixed-tape in middle school? Make a fun play list for yourself – one that is filled with all of your body-moving favorites and take yourself back to your childhood.

3. Go outside. A few deep breaths in the sunshine will flush out energy-draining toxins in your blood stream. Get up from your desk, take the stairs and go outside for 5-10 minutes. Focusing on your breathing and the sunshine penetrating your skin will instantly invigorate. Even on a cloudy day, there is enough vitamin D penetrating the clouds. Going back to your desk by way of the stairs is another benefit.

4. Brighten up. Surround yourself with bright colors. Warm colors (red, orange, yellow) are considered the most energizing, while cool tones (green, blue, purple) are the most calming. Keep a bowl of lemons around and you'll be able to add a zest of citrus and color. Fresh flowers are another great way to bring color and life into your office.

5. Sniff citrus. The scents of oranges, lemons and grapefruits are energizing, waking up your senses. Add a slice or two to a glass of water and refresh and energize yourself any time of day. This is especially great for first thing in the morning since citrus also aids in flushing your system.

6. Drink a glass of water. Dehydration causes fatigue and a glass of water in the afternoon helps boost your hydration levels. For every cup of coffee you consume, alternate with a

glass of water to keep the coffee jitters down. This is a good practice for your evening cocktails, as well. Cut down on the calming effects by drinking one glass of water in between each alcoholic beverage.

7. Sneak a snack. Boost your feel-good hormone (serotonin) with a few grams of carbohydrates. A small cup of microwave popcorn, a handful of almonds or some fresh fruit are all energy boosters.

8. Tote some tea. Instead of drinking caffeine to get you going in the afternoon, enjoy a cup of antioxidant-rich green tea to help rev your metabolism and help you sleep better at night. Caffeine in the afternoon has been shown to affect your sleep patterns at night, feeding the cycle of feeling tired in the afternoon. Change your routine and you'll boost your energy.

9. Laugh! A good laugh will offer you a momentary surge of energy. If there is no one to laugh with, practice this proven technique: Start down at the depths of your belly and laugh out loud. Literally, crack yourself up. Just start laughing and you'll discover that it's easy to repeat and you'll be instantly energized.

10. Be thankful. If you have to be at your desk when your energy is feeling low, rather than return emails, write a few thank you notes. You can't be stressed while you're telling someone how grateful you are. Focusing on gratitude will always change your attitude. Send thank you notes to your favorite customers, to the customer who got away and to the customer you haven't seen in a while. Happy, paying customers is the best energy booster to a quiet afternoon.

5 Ways To Appreciate Your Customers

Appreciation is a wonderful thing. It makes what is excellent in others belong to us as well. - Voltaire

Today, a salesman who just happened to be in my office building visiting one of his own customers visited me. I was impressed by the effort. When you stop in and tell your customers how much you appreciate their business, you give them something to tell others about. I know that there are a lot of sales people who knock on doors and beat the streets for new business, but I wonder, how often do you stop and visit your current customers?

So often, once the transaction is over, your attention quickly moves on to the next customer. You leave your past customers in the dust, while you go looking for that prince of a customer who will make all your sales goals come true. Yet, you already have a customer who values your product. Here is somebody who has already bought into your brand. However, once the sale is over, they never hear from you again. That is, unless you're pitching for another sale. You already know that it's less expensive to retain a current customer versus seeking out a new one, but how do keep your brand in front of a customer without coming off as a pushy nuisance? You're out there kissing a lot of frogs wondering, "where is my prince?" Your prince of a customer is found in the FROGS.

F- Fuss over your current customers. Discover your customer's hot buttons – and fuel them often. Do you know how to get your customer's attention? A friend of mine felt very fussed over when the service attendant pre-set his radio dials when they installed a new radio in his car. This didn't cost the company anything, but my friend has gone on to brag about the car dealership ever since. Use your own gifts and talents to stand out and get your customers to take notice.

R- Reward your customers for referrals. When they introduce you to someone new, offer them a gift that encourages them to do it again. So often, referral bonuses are only paid out if the deal closes – so reward them simply for the introduction. With a few $5.00 gift cards, you can train that behavior to be repeated, and repeated again.

O- Over-deliver, over-exceed, over-do, over-rise, over-reward, over-flow, over-whelm. When your brand shows up in front of your customer, either in person or via email, newsletter or phone call, you give your customers an opportunity to introduce you to someone new. Keeping in contact keeps your brand on the tips of their tongues. Out of sight proves to be disastrous if you are out mind when it comes to referrals. If your customers don't have you on the tip of their tongue at all times, they won't be referring your business.

G- Give your best. Give your customers something that they can't get anywhere else. Get creative. Get crazy. Get your customers to talk about you. Get your customers to brag about you. Keep a journal for one week tracking your buying purchases. What motivated you to spend? What caught your eye and grabbed your attention. Look at your own business through the eyes of your customers – and if you're too close, ask a real customer to help you out. The very best person to ask about what your customers really want from your business is your customer.

S- Surprise your customers. Turn ordinary interactions into a memorable experience. The goal is create moments for your customer to talk about. Create surprises and you will create great customers who turn others onto your brand. I love it when there is a special surprise for me – especially something simple. Watch the video "Joe the Bagger" and you'll learn what you can do today to make a real difference for your customers.

Once you kiss the frogs, you'll discover that your prince of a customer is the one you already have.

10 Tips For Preparing For Business

*Expect the best. Plan for the worst.
Prepare to be surprised. – Denis Waitley*

Procrastination comes naturally, but if you're not even prepared for the day, how can you expect to be prepared for your business?

Here are 10 tips to help you plan for tomorrow before finishing today.

1. Pack your briefcase or computer bag for tomorrows appointments. Restock business cards, company literature, writing pens, flashdrives, all the tools you'll need to handle tomorrow's tasks.

2. Confirm your meetings. Unconfirmed appointments lead to wasted time and disappointment. Confirm the time AND the place. If the appointment is a telephone call, confirm which of you will be 'dialing' the call. When you take a few minutes to confirm your appointments, you'll put your brand right back on the tip of your customer's tongue. This small detail will earn you more referral business in the future because you are seen as someone who cares and pays attention.

3. Download driving directions. Use the technology you have on your phone or on your computer to make sure you have both plan A and plan B for arriving to your location on time – which should be 10-15 minutes early to allow for parking and check-in delays.

4. Pick up your dry cleaning. The last thing you want to be pressed for (no pun intended) is being without your favorite outfit when the media calls at the last minute for an interview. Never put your clothes away in your closet unless they are pressed and ready-for-wear.

5. Fill up the gas tank. Having to stop for gas is an excuse that you should never have to use.

6. Pack change for parking and tolls.

7. Charge your phone and other personal devices. Dropped calls are one thing, but a dead battery is no-excuse.

8. Bring along paper copies of the agenda. If the meeting is an interview, bring along an extra copy of your resume. If you've already sent over a proposal, it's a sign of efficiency if you "happen to have" an extra copy so your guest isn't embarrassed when they are fishing around looking for it.

9. RSVP for events and appointments immediately upon receiving the invitation and put it in your calendar.

10. Write out your note cards to the people you interacted with today and put them in the mailbox. If you put it off, chances are, you'll never write them. How impressed are you when you receive a card in the mail one or two days after you've met

someone? Return the moment by mailing your note cards today.

Being prepared will often tip the scales in your favor if your client is choosing between one or another. Show them that not only can you get the job, but you can do the job.

8 Benefits To Holding A Workshop

I visualize things in my mind before I have to do them. It's like having a mental workshop. – Jack Youngblood

I was having lunch with a friend who owns a landscape design company, Blue Iris Designs. She offers a unique service that combines the benefits of feng shui within your landscape. She was asking me about the benefits of hosting a workshop. When after all was said and done, it wasn't going to earn her a viable income . With all the time she was planning to invest, her question to me was "Is it worth it to hold a workshop?"

I offered her the same sage advice that I received from Marcia McGilley in the Small Business Development Center and added my own two-cents. There are multiple benefits to speaking at a workshop.

First, you get to touch your database multiple times with invitations, announcements, reminders and follow up notes. This puts your brand on the forefront of your customer's minds and gets them thinking about hiring you again or referring you to others. This is great for developing loyal customers.

Second, you can submit a press release to your local paper and online websites. You can write it yourself or hire a professional to discuss the intrinsic value you are prepared to offer the audience.

Third, you can use your notes to create an article on your website, blog or newsletter. You can submit this article to local publication and on social networking sites. It's a good idea to build a relationship with the media because they are always on the lookout for stories. Your story may be the next hot thing to hit the presses.

Fourth, if you record the event, you'll have a CD to sell. You can sell these at future presentations or use them to create passive income on your website.

Fifth, if you videotape the event, you'll have a video to sell. Again, this is another revenue stream you didn't have before.

Sixth, after several presentations, you can gather all those articles and contain them into your first e-book. With some creativity and nurturing, these notes will serve as the backbone for your chapters. There are several publications to help you get an ISBN number and actually create a hardbound book. A book signing is an incredible event to invite people to, and again, put your brand on people's minds.

Seventh, those who attend the workshop are most likely your target market and qualified customers. With a little follow up, those in the audience can easily become your next client.

The eighth benefit to speaking at a workshop is that you become the industry expert whom people call on, refer to and talk about. You set yourself apart from others in your industry and create more visibility for marketing. Your updated blogs add to your search engine optimization.

And as a bonus, by preparing for the workshop, your research keeps you on top of industry changes and you stay relevant.

When you first start out, find a location where you don't have to pay a fee. There are many local businesses who are eager to have new faces in their establishment and they are happy to work with you. Establish a relationship with the manager at local coffee shops, restaurants, bookstores, conference centers, or even hold them at your own office. Consider aligning with another company who has a great meeting space. Ask them to invite people and you'll increase your audience size.

Make sure you spend just as much time inviting people to attend as you do preparing the materials and you'll discover that speaking at workshops are an effective and beneficial way to grow and market your business while creating new streams of income.

7 Tips For Attracting New Customers

*It is a characteristic of wisdom not
to do desperate things. – Henry David Thoreau*

As business owners or sales people looking to attract new sales, you need more tips to attract new customers. You've learned all the tricks and techniques that push customers into making a decision, but when you're pushing your customers, it's easy to feel rejected before you even get started. Chasing customers is tiring – it's way more fun when they chase you.

To create new sales, you have two options. You can fish for new prospects yourself or, you can look to your past customers to help create a new pool of fresh sales. We often overlook the value of past customers because they don't have the same invested interest in growing our business as we do, but they offer a distinct advantage. Because they don't receive any financial compensation, your potential customers know that their testimonial is unbiased and they don't feel pushed. When a potential customer learns about you from an unbiased source, the possibility of turning it into a sale greatly increases. This is a great benefit to "pull" marketing.

Using the Internet is a great way to get your customers to chase you. But you don't have to put all your eggs in one basket. Here are 7 fun ways you can attract new customers to your brand. It's called Push Versus Pull Marketing. There are several blogs out there discussing this very topic.

If you are looking for instant gratification, and can't wait for the radio show, here is list of seven marketing techniques that will pull your customers into your brand versus you pushing your services onto them.

1. Set up your website and match the domain name to your business name. Matching the name makes it easy for customers to find you and to promote you to others. If you aren't the owner of the company or you are competing with other sales people, consider creating your very own personal website. Your website is your store that is open 24 hours a day. Turning your website into a destination that people want to return to and tell others about keeps potential customers returning to you instead of your competition.

2. Create a personal profile and a business presence on social networks such as Facebook and LinkedIn. If all eyes are on social media, you want to make sure your brand has a presence. Read this blog asking the question, are you being found? http://www.shubee.com/buzz/are-you-being-found

3. Your potential customers are reading blogs and this is a great platform to talk about your industry. You don't have to create your own material. Find other blogs and comment on them. This draws attention and potential customers to your brand.

4. Attend networking events to expand your network, not to sell to the people in the room. Create relationships with people you can brag about. They will brag about you, too.

5. Submit your own articles to publications that your target market read. Written articles create visibility and credibility for your brand. Establish yourself as the expert and people will be contacting you.

6. Get involved with Internet radio. Here is an inexpensive medium that puts your message out for all to listen to and enjoy on their own schedule. Shows can be downloaded, podcasted and listened to any time, no matter when it was recorded. If you don't have enough content to start your own show, become a guest on someone else's show who shares the same audience you're after.

7. Use invitations to create a connection. People love to be included. An invitation to an event you are holding or that your trade association is putting together provides multiple opportunities to connect with your customers. The secret to a successful invitation is all in the follow up. Do not drop the ball here.

Stop chasing customers and put your brand in places where they can pull you in on their own schedule. The results are way more fun when your customers chase you.

3 Steps To Extreme Customer Service

I can't get no satisfaction. – Mick Jagger

There are 3 steps to creating extreme customer service. The steps build upon each other to create a great customer experience that gets your customers bragging about you.

1. Go Beyond Satisfaction

2. Get Rid of Sacrifices

3. Generate Surprise

Step One – Go Beyond Customer Satisfaction

Remember that you're after their business for a lifetime, not only a one-time transaction. Your clients aren't looking for a product. Nor are they looking to be sold on anything. They want solutions. They want help. And you are the expert standing in front of them. Do you really know your product or service inside and out? Can you speak intelligently about the value of your product from the customer's point of view?

Use interactive dialogue – When you follow the same tune as an informal conversation, you can find out why the buyer wants the product. You remove yourself from the role of the seller, to someone trying to help because you care. If you listen, the customer will tell you exactly what they want. You can use this information to exceed their expectations.

Sell the features before the product – If the initial conversation focuses on the added value, the customer will use this information to make comparisons – and you're more likely to get the sale.

Pay attention – Use eye contact, smile, speak clearly and look professional.

Be creative and brainstorm with others – This is where the diversity of your team really wins out. The more ideas you share, the faster new ideas seem to come. Creativity and generosity feed each other.

Your customer will rarely be more excited than you are about your product, so your enthusiasm needs to be contagious. You must be passionate and excited about your brand and let go of any limiting beliefs that may be holding you back.

Step Two – Get Rid of Customer Sacrifice

Your success doesn't come from selling. It comes from building relationships. You aren't convincing people to buy something they don't need. Instead, you are creating an easy way to get your product into your customer's hands. Or is it easy?

Walk around your shop during normal office hours and see how many times you say NO to your customers. No parking. No drinks past this point. No large bills. No service. How can you say YES to your customers? Often, when you are generous in small ways, you can impact people's lives forever. When you know that your customer's are going to request gift-wrapping, be ready to provide it. Offer cold bottled water or a comfortable place to sit and look through your catalogs and merchandise. Offer toys for kids and snacks for pets. When you know that your customers will have a long wait, make them feel comfortable and welcome by offering cookies, free wi-fi, or other amenities. When you are knowledgeable about your customers, you are able to provide overwhelming value instead of confusing policies that leave them frustrated.

People buy based on their emotions. People want to feel appreciated. People want to feel like they got a good value. If you can anticipate your client's needs and meet them, you will develop added value and extreme customer service!

Step Three – Generate Customer Surprise

Develop excitement by using creative communication that focuses on the ultimate benefit of your product. If you can surprise them – they will talk about it. Customers will share their surprise with others and invite them to experience the same thing. Your customers will bring others to your store – to your brand – so they can share the memory with someone else.

Here are some great ways to reengage your customers that give them a reason to see your product or service again.

Plan an event. Host a party that brings customers to your door – or puts them in front of your brand. Celebrate a milestone, host a fundraiser, a customer appreciation luncheon – anything that draws in your customers and encourages them to bring a guest along. This is a creative way to draw people into your store. Make sure your product is dressed for success and then follow up with everyone who attends. Send them off with a photo or memorabilia of the event to continue to trigger their experience and their memory. This adds extreme value to your customers and to your brand. Planning creative events are a great way to get customers talking about you.

Personalized Notes – The value of a handwritten card or postcard is strong, especially in today's electronic industry. How often do you receive a personal note? A handwritten note is often one of the first pieces of mail someone will open. Who knows if they will even open your newsletter in the e-mail inbox, but you can almost guarantee they will read your card. What takes you only a few minutes to write may be something that inspires another person to talk about you.

Follow Up – Paying attention to your customers "after" the sale is truly offering extreme customer service. Customers don't expect to hear from you afterward – unless it's for a pitch to sell to them again. Make it a habit to send cards, write emails, make phone calls and extend invitations regularly.

Creating extreme customer service is an on-going process – but the rewards are instant and continuous. Couple these tips with some intentional conversations with your clients. The benefits you and your customers receive will be worth far more than the effort.

7 Ways To Create Extreme Customer Service

Seven is the number of completion. – Biblical Scholars

In a market full of overwhelming choices, competitive prices, and message overload, it seems businesses are finding it more and more difficult to connect with customers in a new and fresh way. Is bigger and faster always better? In a rushed society, sometimes we forget to slow down and realize that our customers are real people, just like us. If we stop and take a deep breath, we can hear the heartbeat of our business – it's our customers. When we spend some time actually listening to our customers, focusing on the person and not just the sale, maybe we can create a loyal customer who brags about our service. The key to extreme customer service is old-fashioned, really; spend time getting to know your customers.

Using these seven avenues, you will connect with your customers, creating extreme customer service and loyal ambassadors for your brand.

Email. Email is the most crowded and overused, but the most expected–so if you're going to send an email – make it personal and never send spam or junk mail. You've all heard my pitch about requesting permission to place someone on your newsletter. I rarely send Eric out with a sledgehammer when someone automatically puts me on their list, but if you don't know the person – it was a drive-by collection of business cards – they don't belong on your list. If it's someone you know, who knows you, has an inkling of interest, then you're probably okay. Use email to send a personal note and share information. E-newsletters are a great way to keep your brand in front of your clients, but they won't build relationships. Follow up an e-newsletter with a phone call for increased effectiveness and conversation. Tips for effective emails: always include your contact information and logo in your signature. If you send something worthwhile, the hope is that your message will be forwarded. Make sure people can contact you. Add a link to your website that offers something of interest or value to the recipient. Once there, have a call-to-action that gets them further into your brand. Do not use email to make a decision or conduct a conversation; too much is left up to interpretation.

Telephone. The telephone, which can sometimes be viewed as weighing 100 pounds, is your link to building rapport. In the age of quick emails, the phone can be a welcome channel for making connections. If you need a quick response, the telephone can often be quicker than email. There are times when you need to make sales calls, but think of your telephone as an additional way to connect with your customers; you're not always calling to make a sales pitch. Make a phone call to say thank you for the meeting, the sale, the introduction or to confirm a meeting or answer questions. Sometimes, your customers need to hear your voice. These conversations can sometimes take on a life of their own and when you let your guard down, you might just learn something that helps you help them, help you help them. Tips for effective phone messages: leave a clear, enunciated message with your phone number. Tell the recipient who you are, why you are calling, and how to respond. An effective voicemail is more likely to be returned. Also, keep your answering message brief, but professionally interesting. We know you can't take our call right now – so bring a smile to my face, if you can. Finally, return phone messages. Call your customers back every time they call you.

Snail mail. Sending a handwritten letter, card or note can go a long way in creating long-term customers and offering extreme customer service. You can almost guarantee that your handwritten card will be opened, especially if it's personal. If your cards are automated or computer-generated, the effect will lose it's luster over time – but a personalized note can make a powerful and positive impact on your customer. I keep a memo board of the cards we receive, and it's about time for a second board. What better pick me up than to read a friendly note from someone who took some time out of his or her busy day to say, "You matter". We all struggle everyday, and a genuine note can really mean a lot. It only takes you a few minutes, but the impact is far greater. If you need some tips on what to say, visit a greeting card website for starters. If you write something genuine, it will be right. A phone call is a great way to follow up this gesture, even an invitation for a cup of coffee. Tips for writing cards: make it personal and hand-written. Include your logo on the envelope or stamp. Remember: birthday cards, anniversary cards, get well cards, thank you's and notes of appreciation. When the postmaster raises prices, send your customers a book of 2-cent stamps. Send cards everyday to people you meet and always send a thank you after the sale.

Face to Face – When your customer is involved in the buying process, you are focused on offering great customer service. But, what are you doing for them "after" the sale or "before" they've decided to buy? A client doesn't care how much you know until they know how much you care. Drop in and visit, set up a coffee date, give them leads, ask them how you can serve them better. Offering to meet with them face to face to catch up, learn more about their needs, just to chat or to offer solutions shows you care enough to spend some time with them. To create extreme customer service, you must care about them as people. Create a conversation and ask them "What do you want me to KEEP doing, to STOP doing or to START doing?"

Memories are built face to face. If you're going to offer extreme customer service, you have to create a memory for your customer to talk about. You need to convert the buying process and every customer interaction into a memorable experience. Do something for your customers that they can't expect anywhere else. The goal is to get your customers bragging about you. Your customers will rarely be more excited about your brand than you are – so you need to be contagious and enthusiastic. Spend time talking with your customers about how you can serve them better – ask them why they chose you over someone else – and then use that information to create an element of customer surprise.

Invitation. Inviting your customers to an event is a great way to re-connect. If it's been a while since they've seen you, heard from you, or purchased from you, invite them to an event. Plan an event of your own or invite them to one that is already happening. Take advantage of the events your community puts together and never go with your passenger seat empty. Take along a customer or two. An invitation is a non-threatening approach to building extreme customer service. It's also a great way to say thank you or create a dialogue with someone you'd like to do business with. Be creative. Make it something you enjoy; sporting events, cultural events, civic events. An even better way to get them into your door, in front of your brand is to create your own gala. Celebrate a milestone, host a fundraiser, make up an excuse to pull people together. Make the presentation as special as you can. Tips for invitations: spend time doing what you enjoy with people you enjoy. You will create very loyal customers when you spend time together. If you are hosting an event, let other's do the work so you can spend time mingling with your guests. You will discover many stories that will strengthen your customer relationships.

Follow Up. Every customer interaction is an opportunity to re-engage them in conversation or bring them further into your sales process. Develop a strategic follow-up plan that is automatic – not automated – that you consistently use. Follow up every conversation, email, or newsletter. When you keep in touch with your customers, they remember to do business with you and they tell others. Satisfied customers will shop around. Unless you keep your brand fresh in your customer's memory, someone else will reap the next purchase. Secure events with a memento of the occasion. Just like souvenirs or vacation photos, a promotional item that complements the occasion will trigger your customer's memory of you long after the event is over. Don't let neglect be the reason your customers shop around. Tips for better follow up: be consistent. Let your customers hear from you all year long, not just when it's time to purchase. Be creative and mix it up. If you always send a survey – add something new to the questions. Give your customers something they weren't expecting.

Rewards. Reward your customers for sharing your name. Be excited when someone sends you a lead. Encourage them to do it again with bribery. If they talked about you once, you can get them to do it again, if you treat them right.

In business, without your customers, you have a very expensive hobby. If you treat customer service as a hobby and don't commit to the daily care and feeding of the heartbeat of our business – then the only heartbeat you will be hearing will be your own.

Your customers are waiting to hear from you – go surprise them.

4 Prospecting Tips For Network Marketing

The only people who aren't involved in network marketing are people who don't understand it. – Mark Segars

After sitting in on a network marketing presentation that dragged on and on, and despite my answers of not being interested, I felt compelled to write some tips for network marketers that keep your prospects in mind. Throughout this presentation, I felt like no one was listening to me. I felt like the only priority was the agenda at hand, and my own interests or goals were irrelevant. I have some prior MLM experience. I understand the background. Combined with my current career of teaching others how to build relationships with customers, I came up with 4 tips to help with prospecting for your network marketing business.

1. Go!

The first tip is to go out and meet people. Go to all the training and seminars – and bring people with you. Go to as many events as possible. Never go anywhere with your passenger seat empty. Take a guest, or a prospect or a customer or a friend. It's really easy to put prospecting on the back burner, but you really need to schedule time for it. If you're spending less than 3 nights per week building your business, you are taking the long route. Don't sit home, GO!

2. It's not about you.

Nobody cares so much about you or why you are building your business. Show your prospects overwhelming value for themselves. Discover their needs, dreams, passions, and goals and see if you can help them achieve them. Don't sell your product or business plan until you've discovered why your prospect would buy it.

• Listen to their story. Your prospects will tell you everything you need to hear, when you listen. Listening will help you to qualify your prospect, keeping you more productive.

This is also a quick way to reconnect later. Remember their story and build on it. Remembering details will keep you connected with them. If you want people to remember you, use a story. Long after facts are forgotten, stories travel.

• Get 3 Yeses. Don't go for open-ended questions. Get them to say YES! This primes your prospect to be in agreement with you. Psychologically, once they say no, you have to work that much harder to bring them back to a place of saying yes to anything, including a next appointment.

• Talk about the value of your business or product. What are the 3 top ways you help people? Share the value and you will connect with people as the expert rather than as a salesperson.

• Create an experience. Nothing bonds people together stronger than a shared memory. Create an experience that will linger in your prospect's memory long enough for them to talk about it, and you will increase your value and demand for your business.

3. Respect Their Time.

Tell your prospect why you are meeting and how long it will take. Don't beat around the topic. Your time and your prospect's time is valuable, and you'll show more respect the clearer you are. If possible, finish the meeting early. Never go longer, even if they seem intrigued. Always schedule another appointment before you leave, even if it's just for coffee.

4. Build relationships with your prospects.

The success of your business is in direct correlation to the relationships you build. Relationships are built face to face and with continual interaction. Follow up your meetings with handwritten cards and phone calls. Use email to share information – not to make decisions or build relationships. Your prospects should hear from you several times per year by phone, and monthly via newsletter or email. They should see your face at least every 4 months. So invite them to share a cup of coffee once in awhile. Keep them included with your business updates. There's no excuse for not staying connected, with email, voicemail, cell phones and social media, there's always a way to get in touch.

Network marketing offers so many opportunities. You get the benefits of a large company backing you, but with the flexibility and tax benefits of owning your own business. It's really easy to focus on the operations side, but when you focus on building relationships with people, your business will grow.

Closing Thoughts

It's that wonderful, old-fashioned idea that others come first and you come second... Others matter more than you do, so don't fuss dear; get on with it. – Audrey Hepburn

As we conclude these articles for now, we hope that you have been sufficiently inspired to put into action the things that you have learned from these pages. This is not the end, but rather just the beginning... It is the beginning of great things for you and your business.

We would love to hear from you, and celebrate in your successes. You may connect with us via the following online outlets:

www.FaceBook.com/ExperiencePros

www.Meetup.com/TheRevolution

www.Twitter.com/ExperiencePros

Experience Pros University

Retain and Gain More Customers with a Proven Method of Word-of-Mouth Marketing

Experience Pros University is a 12-month program. Monthly classes focus on developing relationships with your customers and creating a buzz of marketing for your business.

In each 2-hour class, you will:

- Learn how to focus on the right customers to ensure your marketing efforts are not being wasted.

- Leverage your existing database to create retention, referrals and word-of-mouth marketing.

- Increase your social media presence with our revolutionary method for building brand recognition.

- Create an action plan for reaching potential business and creating brand-loyal customers.

- Incorporate a system that brings more people to your sales process.

Sign up for the next Experience Pros University course at www.ExperiencePros.com

WHAT ARE YOU WAITING FOR? JOIN THE REVOLUTION!

What students of Experience Pros University Are Saying:

"I truly enjoyed being a part of EPU and gained confidence and credibility for gaining and obtaining clients. Throughout the year, I have continually gone back through my EPU manual and refreshed my brain and gained motivation. The book always helped push me forward so thank you for all you did." – Kari Quinn

"It was an honor and a pleasure being a part of EPU." – Ron Skinner

"I enjoyed the training and plan on recommending it to others." – Chris Crary

"Loved the classes. Loved the opportunity I was given to improve the Women's Gym. I know that if I ever have my own business, I would use EPU as a resource for me." – Patty Hepplewhite

Experience Pros Radio Show

Inspiring You to Get Your Business Right!

The Experience Pros Radio Show is your daily in-your-pocket, in-the-car, in-your-office, business training.

Spend time every day discovering your customer's point of view, and how to create a revolution in the way you treat people in business.

- Live on AM 560 KLZ, Monday through Friday, in Denver. Look up your local listings for times. Stream live at www.560TheSource.com.

- Participate in live chat and online conversation during the show on www.Facebook.com/ExperiencePros

- Download podcasts on iTunes or on ExperiencePros.com

What are you waiting for? Join the Revolution!

SUPER-Marketing
Audio Seminar

The How-To Course on Generating Word-of-Mouth Marketing that Out-Performs Your Own Efforts!

This 60-minute audio seminar will teach you:

- Quick and easy ways to market your business

- Healthy business alternatives to marketing

- Common mistakes to avoid

- Where to get the best return on your marketing dollars

SUPER-Marketing is the time-tested, proven-effective system of generating word-of-mouth buzz developed and implemented by Experience Pros, LLC. You will enjoy the banter between Eric and Angel as they take you on an experience-based journey through the super-market! That's right! Your marketing answers can all be found in the four major sections of the grocery store, and your guides will point out each of the items that you SHOULD be doing... and what items you need to put a FREEZE on!

What are you waiting for? Join the Revolution!

Lists That Saved My Life

As a perpetual list-maker and working mom, Angel Tuccy, shares her secrets for balancing family, career and her personal life with the use of *Lists That Saved My Life*.

Discover how Angel takes every day trials and turns them into manageable lists.

Gain valuable insight and helpful tips on:

- Saving Money
- Saving Time
- Running a Household
- Setting Goals
- Gaining Help From Your Family

…And getting all those daily details under control!

Lists That Saved My Life is the very tool all working moms have been waiting for.

You'll find yourself referring back to the *Lists That Saved My Life* again and again.

What are you waiting for? Join the Revolution!

"I recommend that you pick up Angel's book, Lists That Saved My Life. From the moment you crack the cover, you are transported smack into the middle of Angel's life as she and her family are driving home from a camping trip. The entire book is a master's level course in event management told in story form. There's not a single thing in the stories that we can't relate to at a certain level - some of it deeply." – Mark Crowley, KNUS/KRKS Radio

"Angel is a remarkable speaker, trainer and an accomplished author. Her ability to connect with others truly inspires all who come in contact with her to listen to what this exceptional person has to say in regard to the "Extreme Customer Service" skills she, and her partner Eric Reamer, teach. She unquestionably inspires you to strive for your best as she touches you with her truly angelic nature. Any organization would be wise to connect with Angel and Eric, to learn the "Extreme Customer Service" skills they teach." – Rob Hale, Travel-N-Relax

"Lists That Saved My Life is an easy read that everyone should pick up. This book helps you realize which lists are most important, how to organize your busy life, and still manage a good balance of work and family. You will find this book to be very conversational. Angel speaks right to you, and provides tons of amazing insight." – Lindsay Hernandez, BWT Risk Advisors

About The Authors

Angel Tuccy is the best selling author of *Lists That Saved My Life*, *Lists That Saved My Business* and *Sex, Drugs, & Rock N Roll: 3 Keys For A Healthier Lifestyle*. She loves to write, read and travel with her family. For seventeen years, Angel has juggled the roles of working mom and business owner. She's a regular speaker for women's groups and at her local Chamber of Commerce. Angel is a professional-level member of the National Speakers Association, she sits on the board of directors for the Chamber of Commerce of Highlands Ranch and runs a professional women's group called *Ladies Who Lunch*.

Angel and her husband, Jay are the parents of three children. They live in Denver, Colorado.

Eric Reamer is the best selling author of Lists That Saved My Business, and has served in a management capacity for numerous companies, restaurants and non-profit organizations over the course of twenty-five years. He is recognized internationally as a public speaker and professional stage illusionist. He enjoys reading and writing, and anything having to do with coffee. Eric is a professional-level member of the National Speakers Association, and loves training others how to communicate their message more dynamically.

Eric is the father of two sons, and lives in Denver, Colorado.

Together, Eric and Angel are the founders of *Experience Pros University*, and the creators of the audio seminar *SUPER-Marketing* as well as the hosts of a daily radio show in Denver, Colorado, The Experience Pros Radio Show.

Find out more about Eric and Angel at
www.ExperiencePros.com.

www.ingramcontent.com/pod-product-compliance
Lightning Source LLC
Chambersburg PA
CBHW032021170526
45157CB00002B/796